This book is a humble offering at the Divine Lotus Feet of my beloved Lord Sri Sathya Sai Baba. The one who planted the thought and acted upon it too, I pray to thee to also bear the fruits thereof.

SAI, THY KINGDOM COME

A deliberation on the possibility of Sri Sathya Sai Baba's "return"

by
SREEJITH NARAYAN

Blessed indeed are those who will be able to experience that heaven on earth
-*Sri Sathya Sai Baba*

Copyright © Sreejith Narayan

All rights reserved. No part of this book may be reproduced or transmitted in any form or stored in a retrieval system or translated into any language for any means without the written permission of the author, except for brief excerpts or quotations with appropriate credit to this book. Excerpts and quotations used in this book from other books or websites are copyrights of their respective owners and are used herein under the Copyright fair use policy.

ISBN: 978-1492928119

Second Edition - US English - June 2012
First Edition - US English - April 2012

If you like this book or have any comments, questions or concerns, kindly forward them to the author via email to **snarayan@saikingdom.com** or visit the author's website **www.saikingdom.com**.

Contents

FOREWORD 1
ACKNOWLEDGEMENT 11
INTRODUCTION 12
   ABOUT THIS BOOK 13
CHAPTER 1: WAS SWAMI SPEAKING IN LUNAR YEARS? 21
   THE LUNAR YEAR THEORY 21
   THE CASE OF 100 YEAR OLD DEVOTEES 25
   FURTHER EVIDENCE 28
   SWAMI'S BIOGRAPHERS ELUCIDATE 29
CHAPTER 2: WHAT IS HIS PLAN? 31
   DID SWAMI CHANGE HIS PLAN THEN? 31
   SO WHAT IS HIS PLAN? 32
CHAPTER 3: SWAMI TALKS ABOUT HIS LIFETIME ON EARTH .. 34
   ONE POSSIBLE EXPLANATION 37
CHAPTER 4: SAI PREDICTIONS FOR THE FUTURE 39
   WE HAVE NO BUSINESS TO DOUBT 42
CHAPTER 5: CLUES FOR HIS IMMINENT RETURN 47
   A MIRACLE TO COME 49
   DREAMS OF DEVOTEES 52
CHAPTER 6: INCREDIBLE NADIS 60
   PROPHECIES ABOUT SATHYA SAI AVATAR IN NADIS 60
   MY EXPERIENCE WITH NADIS 67
   NADIS PREDICT SWAMI'S RETURN 68
   INTRIGUING NOSTRADAMUS PROPHECY 72
CHAPTER 7: THE DISAPPEARANCE OF MAHDI 75
   WHO IS MAHDI? 75
   SIGNS TO IDENTIFY MAHDI 75
   MAHDI'S REIGN ON EARTH 79
   MAHDI'S DISAPPEARANCE 81
   WHEN WILL MAHDI RETURN? 84
   MAHDI TO BE BACK IN A YOUNG BODY? 85

THE GOLDEN AGE OF MAHDI 86
WHY WILL MAHDI RETURN? 88

CHAPTER 8: A VISION IN THE SKY? 89

VISWARUPA DARSHANAM POSTPONED 93
STORM BEFORE THE CALM? 97
A WALK ACROSS THE SKY 98

CHAPTER 9: DAWNING OF THE SATHYA SAI GOLDEN AGE ... 103

THE GOLDEN AGE WILL RECUR 105
SIGNIFICANCE OF THE YEAR 2012 112
THE GOLDEN AGE ACCORDING TO SCRIPTURES 113
COMING OF THE SON OF MAN 117

CHAPTER 10: WHY DID SWAMI LEAVE HIS BODY? 124

THIS BODY HAS COME FOR THE SAKE OF DEVOTEES 124
THE POWER OF PRAYERS 134
NEWS THAT TRAVELLED FAR AND WIDE 136
MANY THINGS IN ONE STROKE 138

CHAPTER 11: THE GLORY OF RESURRECTION 140

QUESTION OF A BODY 143
THE CONCEPT OF NIRMANA KAYAS 145

CHAPTER 12: CONCLUSION 149

SWAMI WILL KEEP ALL PROMISES 152
A TRAINING PERIOD FOR HIS DEVOTEES? 154
SAI, THY KINGDOM COME… 159

PRAYER 160

BIBLIOGRAPHY AND REFERENCES 162

Foreword

By Jody Cleary and Ted Henry

Without giving away its thesis, I will say that "*Sai, Thy Kingdom Come*" by Sreejith Narayan is a great read. And that is certainly the least of it.

The author's calm, measured, irrefutably logical and impeccably researched presentation is beyond reproach. If one follows carefully to its conclusion, this book's premise is something one cannot easily ignore or forget, no matter what one's biases are.

As for myself and my husband, Ted Henry, Sri Sathya Sai Baba has not skipped a beat in His interaction with us. His amusing leelas, lessons and dreams and Divine Presence remain as constant after the *Mahasamadhi* as before. Our Souljourns Seva and love for Him are redoubled, if anything. He has done for us and given to us more than we could or would have ever imagined or asked. We are permanently submerged in overwhelming gratitude.

And yet...though Ted and I could ask for nothing more, what about those who did not have the opportunity to enjoy Him and benefit?

And yet...the world situation seems to require some even more drastic shock to arrest its current trajectory and to transform this world into "One vast loving kin" as our Swami once predicted.

And yet...it was a relief to have "*Sai, Thy Kingdom Come*" put words put to many of our hidden thoughts, questions, unvoiced secret suspicions.

And we have learned from experience that we surely must love His "uncertainty".

And above all, nothing is beyond Him!

We would all only rejoice if graced to witness the individual and world transformation that would inevitably ensue if what Sreejith Narayan so carefully and courageously suggests in "*Sai, Thy Kingdom Come*" is part of The Golden Age, the Sathya Yuga.

[Jody Cleary and her husband Ted Henry from USA, are long-time devotees of Sri Sathya Sai Baba. Ted Henry has been a Television journalist for more than 40 years. He recently retired from WEWS-TV, the ABC affiliate in Cleveland, Ohio, USA where among his many duties, he presented a weekly news report on spirituality called, "Heart and Soul". Ted and Jody have traveled extensively for the past 15 years conducting video interviews with Sai devotees and other spiritual aspirants. These videos are made available to all through their Souljourns websites:

www.vimeo.com/souljourns
www.youtube.com/souljourns
www.souljourns.net]

Foreword

By Jullie Chaudhuri

Sai Thy Kingdom Come...the line which subsequently follows this significant prayer statement is - **Thy Will be done.** Beloved Bhagawan's Will is Supreme. His Kingdom will come as and when He Wills it so! For our part, we need to exercise patience and await the unfolding of events, so extraordinaire, that generations hence for eons to come will speak of it in absolute awe.

The power-packed pages of this compilation opens in such a gripping manner, that one is compelled to read on, savoring each nuance that chooses to make an appearance therein. **The author quite emphatically states, that this book does not attempt to predict what is going to happen, it advertently takes the shape of an academic research.** It is indeed a thorough chronology of Bhagawan's declarations, synchronizing with His advent, going on to encompass many decades. And naturally His affirmations, being the words of Truth - enhances solace and refuels hope. **The section of texts, scrupulously reproduced from age-old Nadi scriptures, documented personally by ancient seers and sages, are a wondrous revelation.** Though, there is nothing more enlightening that can be said, yet the topic is such that feelings gush forth, seeking expression.

Can one ever forget 24th April 2011? For almost a month Bhagawan had chosen to "confine" Himself within the Temple of Healing that He had personally founded - the SSSIHMS at Prasanthigram. With bated breath, tears of anguish, passionate appeals and fervent prayers, devotees the world over united to beseech their Beloved

One to heal Himself, to return to Yajur, to resume *Darshans*. But, Bhagawan had His own plans and it had to unfold as per His Will. His ways are known only to Him - unfathomable and infinite, beyond the human mind that is frail, frivolous and finite. It is not within the purview of our limited intelligence and colored vision, to decipher and comprehend what He chooses to take upon Himself, selflessly and unconditionally for the purpose of Individual as well as Cosmic benefit. His departure from physical devastated devotees across the globe, wrecking the psyche, flooding it with turmoil. How can this be true? How can He leave like this? Surely this is a nasty nightmare? Snatched away from life was its melody, with one stroke the rhythm had bid adieu. The mind was swathed with questions, the shattered heart buried in agony, overwhelmed by a tsunami of grief and the soul appeared flightless in a deep void.

The intellect knows whatever takes a form has to merge back into formlessness. Once born into the material realm, the soul has to depart from it too, but something seemed amiss here. A feeling kept gathering momentum – there is more to come. The era of Sathya Sai certainly has much more in store. **His entrance was so spectacular, so unique. His exit, when the time does come, will be equally so, for He is the source of all Avatars. This is an interval, a Divine Intermission**. This hiatus, this pause is a time to intensify our efforts and spiritual practices. It is an interlude for in-depth individual and collective *sadhana* (spiritual endeavor) to complete our homework, to work upon ourselves in order to graduate. So also, this is the phase, to ruminate, to pledge, to rededicate, to affirm and reaffirm our willingness to serve Him in all of creation. **And, with the intensity of collective thought process, gather a "Critical Mass" seeking the cherished return of Beloved Bhagawan.**

Foreword

Since nothing happens without the Will of the Lord, this manuscript - Sai Thy Kingdom Come, this colossal outpour from the author's heart, mind and soul, has been so inspired by Divine Design. **Such expansive research into Beloved Bhagawan's words is a feat that has been accomplished only through His Grace alone! And the time too, has been selected by Bhagawan, the Master Planner, to herald in that Critical Mass, through "Sai Thy Kingdom Come".** What was earlier spoken about in hushed whispers, not meant for everyone's ears; the hopes, visions and dreams, the longing and the yearning, the firm faith and the total conviction, has come into the open. **And to "Sai Thy Kingdom Come" accrues the blessed credit of such an occurrence.** Sreejith, has with supreme dedication carried out a meticulous research. Every word, each line, all the pages appear so fluid, riveting one's attention completely. **It's all about His word, the message in each word, the truth laden in each word, the word of Truth, of Sathya...the Sathya of Sai!**

Just how this Divine Drama unfolds is entirely up to Him. Yet, our intention, our belief, our conviction, our dedication, our faith and devotion is within our grasp. We each have our own Universe and what we draw into that Universe is up to us. There is no such thing as impossible for our Lord, Whose Will defies all things finite, it is His script after all! Even as we await and wait, let us refrain from debate; silently reflect, ponder and deliberate, upon Him and His words. Let us come together, form a link, suffuse it with clear intent and pure love, allow compassion to reign supreme and pray for the unfolding of that event which will benefit the cosmos through an age golden and true. This book wonderfully assimilates and assembles Bhagawan's proclamations from innumerable texts under "one roof", so to say, for easy reference.

While perusing through, one will appreciate how often Bhagawan has avowed that His words will never fail; what He has planned must succeed; His activities and movements can never be altered; He will never deviate from His word; though owing to compulsion of circumstances some changes may take place, but they are not permanent and will not change His course; that the golden age will recur in the era of Sathya Sai and will be heralded by a new coming; a day of awakening, a revelation of the true power of God.

Let us plead and implore Beloved Sai to will His Kingdom to come through soon. Let us entreat Him to make us worthy and deserving.

Boundless though is He,
Bound to His word is He,
Bound by His devotees,
Bound to return soon is He,
Thereby ending this Divine drama of Samadhi!

Samastha Lokaah Sukhino Bhavantu.

[Sri Jullie Chaudhuri is a proficient writer of high credentials who has written and published numerous articles and poems about her beloved Lord Sri Sathya Sai Baba. She was fortunate to come to the Sai fold at a very young age. For the past 10 years she has been serving as a writer and editor for Sri Sathya Sai Newsletter for Pune Youth Wing. She was blessed to dedicate a book of 85 poems titled "Mother Sai" at His Divine Lotus Feet in November 2010]

Foreword

By Captain Jatindar Shad

To the devoted, the splendor of presence of his or her Chosen God can never be equated with anything else in all the worlds. The God whom you have worshipped with devotion and love, when He leaves His body, there is pain in the heart. But when you get a chance to read of His Return, you read through from beginning to end, without a break!

Sai, Thy Kingdom Come, **is a unique research paper – It cuts across religions and studies all that is available and the pointers are there in each and every religion, although they do not refer to Him as Sai Baba, but as Mahdi or Messiah.**

Any person who knows about Sri Sathya Sai Baba and has a small 2" x 2" picture of Him on his or her home altar, is qualified to read this book and get the joy that I got from reading it.

I greet the Author of this book for a job well done. **No doubt in my mind anymore. He will be back!** – just wait and pray.

Yes indeed this gives confidence to hope. We eagerly await the return of our Beloved Lord - the mankind is yet to be given some directions.

And as we await His return, what can be expected from us? Yes we can strive to become better from what we are right now.

Be in Constant Integrated Awareness of His presence all around you.

Sai Ram – Rejoice!

[Captain Shad was introduced to Sri Sathya Sai Baba while serving in the Indian Army. He left Army as a Captain in 1981 and since then he has been involved in various Seva activities. In 1985 Swami graciously granted him interview and also allowed his team to paint the Prasanthi Mandir. Swami also guided him to make the first ever hologram of Baba in 1990, which was followed by the first ever embossed foil picture of Baba]

About the Author

Sreejith Narayan came into Swami's fold in 1992 and since then Swami has been guiding him in many ways through dreams and life lessons. A Software Engineer by profession, he currently resides in New Jersey, USA and originally hails from Kerala, India. He is currently serving as the Service Coordinator for Bridgewater Sai Center, regularly participates in Sai activities and is very active in the Sai community in his region. Before moving to USA in 1997, he was an active Young Adult and *Sevadal* in Kerala, India.

He always had a wish to write a book about Swami even though he never fully believed in his capabilities to do so. He had expressed his wish to Swami in a letter in 1997 before moving to USA. Swami Graciously accepted it, slapped gently on his hands very lovingly and Sreejith also received *Padanamaskar*. He had collected many quotes and references from various sources for that book. But his wish never got fulfilled for various reasons until during the end of January 2012 when he had a sudden urge to write about Swami's possible reappearance. After that everything came into place one by one and the book came out with Swami's Divine Grace. The research he had done for his other book helped him immensely for this effort. When Swami blesses a letter, He makes it happen too. Such is our dear Lord's love for His devotees as we all know.

In this book, the author proudly compares his convictions to that of a loyal disciple because according to the ancient Indian tradition a disciple always trusts his Guru's words completely, even to the last letter. Such is the conviction and faith that the author has in Swami's words and believes without any doubt that all of them will come true.

Acknowledgement

[...] Do not thank Me. I am not a third person. Do you thank your mother who serves you food every day? You may thank an outsider from whom you receive a favour, but I am not an outsider. So, never say thanks to Swami. Consider Swami as your own. Only then will you have the right to approach Swami.
- Sathya Sai Speaks Volume 31 Chapter 45

My dearest Swami, I am not thanking You since I am Your own and so is this work. Many have contributed to this book; I am not thanking them either for they are my own too. Even in the awareness that You alone are the doer, there could have been moments where ego crept in leading to mistakes. If so, I sincerely pray for Your forgiveness and request the readers to look beyond any shortcomings.

The legend goes that by the mere touch of Saint Jnaneshwar[1], a buffalo started reciting Vedas. The meaning of the name Jnaneshwar is "God of all knowledge", that is to say Swami Himself. I am not trying to recite Vedas. However, I understand that it is impossible to even attempt to write a single word about Him without His Divine Grace. With most reverential salutations I prostrate at the Divine Lotus Feet of my beloved Lord Sri Sathya Sai Baba, the bestower of all knowledge, wholeheartedly praying this *dunnapothu²* may be touched.

---

[1]Sri Jnaneshwar (1275-1296) was a 13th century Indian (Maharashtrian) Saint, poet, philosopher whose commentary on Bhagavad-Gita popularly known as "Jnaneshwari" and the work "Amrutanubhav" are considered to be milestones in Marathi literature.

²As Swami lovingly chides His devotees sometimes. Meaning he-buffalo in Telugu.

Introduction

> Aum Sri Sai Ram
>
> Loving Sairams to the dear reader,
>
> Please note that this book is mainly meant for the devotees of Sri Sathya Sai Baba and assumes that the reader already knows in considerable detail about the Sathya Sai Avatar. The views expressed are solely personal and do not necessarily reflect the views of any group or organization.

Will Swami "return"?

Yes, I do not have any doubt whatsoever!

All of us Sai devotees have faith in Swami's future Avatar as Prema Sai Baba. **But the "return" I am talking about is His reappearance in the same physical form of Sri Sathya Sai Baba.**

What makes me think so?

Swami's words will never fail. Whatever He has said is bound to happen. With that certainty, everything else becomes irrelevant. In the subsequent chapters you will see His words that provide clear indication that it was not time for His final disappearance yet. You will also see why there cannot be any change in Swami's plans either. As far as I am concerned, these would mean only one thing. That He will certainly be back!!! Swami has also provided

Introduction 13

some astounding indications on His imminent return. Further, there are some mindboggling prophecies in certain unique scriptures that clearly foretell Swami's reappearance. Please read on...

About this book

On Sunday April 24th 2011 at around 2:00 AM[1] I was woken up from deep sleep by a phone call. A Sai brother had called to break the shocking news. As my spirit sunk into anguish, heart began to palpitate out of control. Suddenly I felt someone patting on my right shoulder as if to console me. I turned around to acknowledge my wife thinking that it was she, only to find her sitting much further away. Immediately I realized that it was He and a strange sense of calm whelmed me over.

When we look back to that grievous moment I am sure we all can find His unseen hand helping to get each one of us through. It could have been in the form of a touch or a dream or a vision or even through the calming words of another Sai devotee or a family member. Could it be anything, it is only with great awe and amazement that I can bethink of the boundless Love and Grace that made sure each and every one of His devotees survived the shock.

During those few days after Swami "left" many thoughts had passed through my mind. I could not accept that Swami could leave just like that. That too, much before the predicted time. Every devotee I talked to was hopeful of a miracle and there was a general feeling that Swami may resurrect Himself. Soon that hope too faded away as the body was laid to rest in His *Mahasamadhi*. In the

---

[1] US Eastern Time.

meantime some of the television news channels propagated a story of how Swami had mentioned to some of His students that He would be indisposed for a period of 40 days and would return after that. This was said to be written in a book called *Thapovanam*. I immediately acquired a copy of the book and literally swept through it. But I could not find anything of that sort mentioned in that book. Soon devotees started coming up with all sorts of theories about how Swami had already fulfilled His prophecy that He would live 96 years. I found explanations that Swami could have been talking in lunar years and not regular calendar years. It was a "somewhat" convincing theory that everyone could hold on to. After all Swami can never be wrong. But when I analyzed carefully I could see that there was no way Swami could have been speaking in lunar years. I found some of Swami's own words that convinced me that He was not. Mystery still remained.

Now when I look back and reflect on those few days I understand that my thought process was driven by emotions than reasoning. Even reasoning could not have helped since Swami is beyond that as well. Whatever Swami does is beyond our understanding. Why then ask questions? I realized that all I had to do was to just "be". With or without body Swami is always with us. Disappearance of the body in one way has helped me take my baby steps towards going beyond the form and try to see Him in each and everything. May be that is the whole purpose of this drama, to make His devotees rise above the body attachment. His body was just a projection into Prasanthi Nilayam from some unknown realm like a hologram or *"maya"* if I may, so that Divine could interact with humans. Even the disappearance of the same can be considered only as incomprehensible as itself ever was!

Introduction 15

> *The Mahasakthi (Divine Energy) puts on the cloak of Mayasakthi [illusory energy and its forms] in order to fulfill the purpose of contacting and protecting mankind.*
> - Sathya Sai Speaks Volume 1 Chapter 30
>
> *I have to put on Maya Shakthi to come into your midst, like the policeman who is compelled to wear the dress of the thief so that he can get entry into the gang of thieves to apprehend them and bring them to book! The Lord cannot come down with His Maha Shakthi unimpaired; He has to come with diminished splendor and limited effulgence, so that He can become the object of Bhakti and Dedicated Service.*
> - Sathya Sai Speaks Volume 1 Chapter 3

This book is not about trying to understand Swami and His inscrutable ways. Even sages and advanced souls have tried and failed to understand the nature of His reality. Who am I to try? But what I am certain of is that Swami's words cannot fail. There cannot be any changes in His plan either. Not that it really matters. Because He alone knows what is best for this world. Saving the world is Swami's problem really. Who am I to worry? If only I can follow His teachings and save myself, that would be one less problem for Him to deal with! Swami has already left a wealth of teachings in the simplest language possible that even the most ordinary of men can understand the key to attain the zenith of his own existence namely the liberation. What more is left to teach if and when He comes back?

Nevertheless, that does not stop me from believing that it was not time for Him to disappear from this world. Swami's own statements that I found in numerous discourses substantiate my belief. If it was not time for Him to leave yet then it must also be true that He would come back. I have found many Sai devotees including erstwhile students of SSSIHL[1] who share the same belief.

I did not have any plans to write this until about the end of January 2012 when I felt a sudden urge to put an article together on the possibility of Swami's reappearance. I talked about this to a Sai devotee friend and he too encouraged me to write. He told me about a beautiful dream that he had about Swami's reemergence. I also learnt about a few other devotees who had similar dreams about Swami's "return". As I started to look further some astonishing clues emerged. I felt His unseen hand working. The manner in which I received various materials for this work can be deemed nothing less than a miracle. What started as an article became so elaborate that I had to call it a book!

This is not an attempt to predict what is going to happen. It advertently takes the shape of an academic research of which the underlying principle is "He said so, it must happen so". It can also be looked upon as a humble attempt to put together bits and pieces of information into a definite shape and present it before an earnest enquirer. Swami's mystery cannot be understood. The best we can do is to get immersed in it. The only thing certain is that whatever He has said is bound to happen. There is no doubt about it. But He alone knows how since there are many possibilities. A few years from now we would all be able to look back in amazement and admire how everything had come about just the way He had pronounced. But as of now what I am considering in my own limited human capacity is just few of such

---

[1] Alumni of Sri Sathya Sai Institute of Higher Learning.

possibilities. Even though the main source of information has been Swami's discourses, I have also looked into credible information from some books about Him. Other information I have considered include experiences of some eminent devotees, Nadi readings in which I have immense belief by the virtue of personal experience and prophecies that are part of some religious scriptures. More than anything, it is my own conviction in the words of my Guru and God Sri Sathya Sai Baba that has led to this book.

> *My purpose can be understood in a general way only by earnestly and vigilantly watching, trying to get to the meaning of every word and action with patient attention.*
> - Sathya Sai Speaks Volume 29 Chapter 29

That is exactly what I have tried to do. I have looked earnestly for clues in His discourses and tried to get to the meaning of His words with patient attention. I would like to assure the readers that this is not a futile attempt of a lost soul desperately trying to reconcile with his Guru's passing away. Rather I request you to look upon this as the convictions of a loyal disciple who trusts his Guru's words more than his own eyes.

> *The Grace that makes the dumb to speak*
> *And the lame to climb up the peak*
> *Cause be of my earnest feat*
> *That I place at Thy Lotus Feet*

PART I

"My Word will never fail"

CHAPTER 1:
Was Swami speaking in lunar years?

After Swami left His body, the whole Sai fraternity has been looking out for explanations for His early disappearance. Swami can NEVER be wrong. Whatever He has said WILL take place. So it is only natural to assume when Swami left at the age of 85 (84 years and 5 months to be precise) much earlier than the predicted age of 96, that He must have been talking with respect to some other calendar system such as the lunar calendar (or lunar years). When I first heard about this I was also inclined to adopt it as a possibility. But as I looked into various details including Swami's words about His lifespan, it became clear enough to be fully convinced that Swami was not speaking in terms of lunar years. If Swami was not speaking in lunar years then it must be true that He has left earlier than predicted. If so, given that Swami's prediction would eventually be fulfilled, it is possible that He would return in the same form. In fact that is the thinking which has triggered my research and eventually led to this book.

The lunar year theory

Many Sai devotees believe that Swami talked about His life-span with respect to the traditional Hindu (or Indian) lunar years. I found the following explanation floating around in the internet:

> Here is a discussion of Swami's age when He left His body.

In His discourse of 9 September 1960 (Chapter 31 of Sathya Sai Speaks volume 1), Swami said,

"I will be in this mortal human form for 59 years more and I shall certainly achieve the purpose of this Avatar; do not doubt it. I will take My own time to carry out My Plan so far as you are concerned. I cannot hurry because you are hurrying. I may sometimes wait until I can achieve ten things at one stroke; just as an engine is not used to haul one coach, but awaits until sufficient haulage in proportion to its capacity is ready. But My Word will never fail; it must happen as I will."

That would mean that Swami would give up His body at the age of 93 or 94, since He was born on 23 November 1926. But He gave up His physical form on 24 April 2011 (Easter Day) at 7:40AM, at the age of 84. What is the explanation for this seeming discrepancy? Here is one possible explanation.

Swami may have been talking in lunar years, not solar years. Here is a quick calculation, using information found on the internet. Swami lived 30,833 days. **Lunar months average 27.21 days, and there are 12 lunar months in a lunar year. Thus, Swami lived about 1133 lunar months, or 94.4 lunar years. So in that sense He was 94 when He left His body**.

Now let us try to dissect the above explanation. Even though the Hindu calendar month consists of more than 27.21 days (explained later), just for the sake of an argument let us use this number for our calculation. The above explanation about Swami's age at the time of His leaving the physical form would have been appropriate

CHAPTER 1: Was Swami speaking in lunar years?

had He mentioned in the above discourse that He would live 94 years. If that was the case it could be argued that 94 lunar years equals to 84 standard years (of the widely used Gregorian calendar) that Swami actually lived in His body. But what Swami actually said was *"I will be in this mortal human form for 59 years more"*. So the lunar year calculation has to be applied only to those 59 years and not the total 94 years as in the above explanation. Swami made this statement on September 9, 1960. Swami left His body on April 24, 2011. Between those dates, Swami was in His body for 18,489 days. Does this amount to 59 lunar years? Let us check.

A. Number of days in lunar year = 27.21 days x 12 months = 326.52 days. Thus 18,489 days amounts to: 18,489 / 326.52 = 56.63 lunar years (around 57 years)

As shown above, this period amounts to only around 57 years. So what should we reckon? Swami was two years short on His prediction?

But we are not done yet. Just over a year later Swami made a similar statement:

> *You will witness Puttaparthi becoming a Madhura Nagara (birth place of Krishna). No one can stop this development or delay it. I will not give you up, nor can any one of you give Me up. Even if you lose faith, you will repent and come to this refuge very soon, clamouring for admission.* **I shall be in this body for 58 years more; I have assured you of this already.** *Your lives are intertwined with My earthly career. Act always in accordance with that great privilege.*
>
> - Sathya Sai Speaks Volume 2, Prasanthi Nilayam, October 21, 1961

As seen in the quote above, on October 21, 1961 Swami pronounced that He would be in His body for 58 years more.

> B. After making the above statement Swami was in His body for 18,082 days. If we apply the same lunar year calculation as earlier, this amounts to only around 55.4 lunar years. Now we are almost three years short!

Then again there is a larger issue of Hindu calendar month being more than 27.21 days. According to Hindu calendar, a month is 29 days 12 hours and 44 minutes long. If we apply this number to the above calculations, the difference will be substantial! For example, 18,489 days (see above) will be 52.2 years, a difference of almost 7 years (from 59 years in Swami's statement).

The assumption of 27.21 days in a lunar month comes from the convention of nodal months; that is the period in which the Moon returns to the same node of its orbit (nodes are the two points where the Moon's orbit crosses the plane of the Earth's orbit). On an average that duration is about 27.21 days. These correspond to the 27 *nakshatras* of the Hindu calendar month but not to the number of days in a month (Same *nakshatras* could repeat within a given month). Nevertheless, even if we use this number for our calculation, it still does not add up due to reasons mentioned in calculations A and B above that shows a difference of around 2 and 3 years respectively.

So it is clearly evident that Swami was not speaking in terms of lunar years.

The case of 100 year old devotees

Another popular reason for the belief of Swami using lunar years is that He had referred to some of His long-lived devotees as to have "lived hundred years" even though they had not. For example, the great Sri Ghandikota Subrahmanya Sastry, famous Sanskrit pandit and devotee of Swami to whom the Sai Gayatri was revealed, merged in Swami at the age of 93. However Swami remarked to Sri Sastry's grandchildren that their grandfather was a maharishi who had attained the age of hundred (even though he was 93). Swami had also mentioned this in one of His discourses. During another discourse Swami mentioned a prominent devotee Sri Seshagiri Rao who had passed away in his seventees[1] also to have lived hundred years.

> Dr. Padmanabhan's father, Seshagiri Rao came here at the age of 63 after his retirement. He also lived for 100 years and had a peaceful death.
>
> - Sathya Sai Speaks Volume 36 Chapter 20

He mentions about the same devotee in another discourse:

> Earlier, there was Seshagiri Rao in Prasanthi Nilayam. He was a great officer. He used to offer Aarati. He lived for a 100 years.
>
> - Divine Discourse, Prasanthi Nilayam, August 22, 2001

---

[1]According to an article in RadioSai, Sri Seshagiri Rao first saw Swami in 1943 when he was 58 years old. From another source, Sri Seshagiri Rao passed away in 1961. So he must have been 75 to 76 years old.

If we just consider these instances (of Sri Sastry and Sri Rao) separately in isolation, we may be tempted to believe that Swami could have been using a different calendar system for His calculations. That this is not the case is quite evident from the fact that two different ages have been equated to hundred years. Moreover, where are we going to find a calendar that can absorb more than twenty years of difference[1] into its cycles as in the case of Sri Seshagiri Rao?

Among the other devotees whom Swami had mentioned in the discourses to have attained hundred years were Sri Gopal Rao and Swami Karunyananda; both of them actually lived more than 100 years. It should be interesting to note that Sri Gopal Rao was alive and was 96 years old when Swami made that statement about him. Four years later in December 2007 on Sri Gopal Rao's actual 100th birthday, Swami honored this grand old devotee in a felicitation ceremony.

To understand what Swami really meant by the expression "lived hundred years", we need to look into the context in which He made the statements. For that we need to look no further than the same discourse (as mentioned above) on His 78th birthday where He says:

> *I want to tell you another important thing. Here, in Prasanthi Nilayam, all the devotees who dedicate their lives to Swami live for full 100 years.* **Kasturi came here and lived a full life.**
> - Sathya Sai Speaks Volume 36 Chapter 20

We all know that Prof. Kasturi merged in Swami at the age of 90. If we closely examine the above statements we

---

[1] Between 100 years in Swami's description and the actual age of Sri Seshagiri Rao.

CHAPTER 1: Was Swami speaking in lunar years?

can clearly understand that "to live for hundred years" was just an expression that Swami used in order to denote that the devotee had lived a "full life". What does Swami expect from a devotee who lives until the age of 100?

> *At age 100, one should be master of the five working organs and the five sense organs, and should be merged with God. The five working organs are talking, walking, rejecting (excrement), procreating and eating. The five sense organs are hearing, touch, sight, taste and smell.*
>
> - Conversations with Sathya Sai Baba, Dr.John Hislop, SSSBPT, Page 42

Any devotee who has lived a full life and reached the above expectation of Swami, irrespective of their actual age, in absolute spiritual sense would have lived 100 years. Many places in India especially in villages, elders use the expression "May you live for 100 years" to bless their younger ones. It just means "to live a long and fulfilling life". The origin of this expression can be traced to the Vedic blessing *"Shatam Jeevat"* which means "long live" and the *mantra "Jeevam Sharadah Shatam"*, a prayer for longevity. The Sanskrit word *"shatam"* in its numerical sense would denote the number 100 but it also contextually means "a long time". The meaning of the full *mantra* is thus: "Let the faithful live a long, complete, healthy and contented life". I would like to borrow the words of Sri Paramahamsa Prajnanananda of The Kriya Yoga Institute on the real meaning of *"Shatam Jeevat"*: *"A span of 100 years is a symbol of completeness. It is not just a physical number; it symbolically tells us to live a life of love and devotion. In the number 100, if 1 is missing, then*

00 have no value. Similarly, if God or love is missing, life has no value"[1].

These old-time devotees of Swami being such exemplars of love and devotion, in all capacities would have lived a full and complete *"shatam"* years of life that they at some point or the other had surrendered completely to the service of the Divine Lotus Feet!

Further Evidence

Let us examine the following words of Swami on His 79th birthday:

> *Today is the birthday of this body only. Do I look like a **79 years old** person? Not at all!! People at this age get so many ailments. Their ears become weak of hearing, eyes develop cataract, wrinkles form on the forehead. For Me, all the organs are perfectly normal. You will not find any wrinkles on My forehead. Not just now, **even at the age of 80 or even 90**, I will be like this only!!!*
>
> - Divine Discourse, Prasanthi Nilayam, 79th Birthday, November 23, 2004

Since Swami mentions "79 years old" on His 79th birthday, at least in this case it is certain that Swami was speaking in terms of regular (Gregorian) calendar years. Please note the mention of age 90 in the same discourse which clearly means that He intends to be in His body beyond 90 "regular calendar years".

---

[1] Source - www.kriya.org.

CHAPTER 1: Was Swami speaking in lunar years?   29

Swami's biographers elucidate

Late Sri Ra.Ganapati was a very close devotee of Bhagawan and a deep scholar of scriptural texts in various languages. He has authored a biography series named "Baba: Satya Sai" which is considered a magnificent tribute to the life of Bhagawan Sri Sathya Sai Baba. Following is an incident mentioned in one of the volumes:

> His (Swami's) college students had the privilege to see another unique creation in the Ootacamund Summer Course in **June 1976**. Svami, who declared that **He would live to see ninety six years in this body**, mentioned that eighteen important institutions would be established by Him all over India **in the remaining forty six years** [...]
>
> - Baba: Satya Sai Part 2, Ra.Ganapati, Page 85

What needs to be noted here is that Swami not only mentions that He would live until 96 but also indicates He would be present for 46 years after 1976. Swami was 50 at that time and that is why He talks about the *"remaining 46 years"* of total 96 years. Since He indirectly acknowledges His actual age at that time in regular calendar years, it is only logical to assume that the 96 and 46 years mentioned are also in regular calendar years. He could not have been using two different calendars at the same time. Moreover, after 1976 (till 2011) Swami was in His body only for 35 years. It is quite obvious that 35 standard calendar years cannot be equivalent to 46 years of any calendar[1], let alone a lunar one.

---

[1] That would take a calendar with only 23 days a month or 276 days in a year.

Perhaps the most convincing evidence of all can be found in the words left behind by none other than the great (late) Prof. Kasturi, the illustrious chosen biographer of the Divine life-story:

> *Baba has assured us that He will remain in the human frame **beyond the year 2020**.*
> - The Life of Bhagavan Sri Sathya Sai Baba, Kasturi.N, 1971, Page 235

Fortunately for us, by stating a year instead of an age, Swami through His most distinguished messenger Prof. Kasturi has sealed this debate once and for ever giving no scope for even double entendre!

CHAPTER 2:
What is His plan?

In the previous chapter we already saw that Swami was not speaking in lunar years.

Did Swami change His plan then?

So what happened? Why this discrepancy? Did Swami change His original plan and decide to leave early?

When asked about this, some devotees even say "Swami can change His plan any time". Of course, He can! He is Avatar. He is God. He is capable of doing anything He wants to. **But what I do not understand is the wisdom in accusing the Avatar of not foreseeing the "supposed" change to His own plan!** That too, after listening to His umpteen assertions to the contrary? The ones of the following kind?

My Word will never fail; it must happen as I will.

- Sathya Sai Speaks Volume 1 Chapter 31

What I will, must take place; what I plan must succeed.

- Sathya Sai Speaks Volume 12 Chapter 38

Once My Word goes forth, it must happen accordingly. Do not doubt it.

- Sathya Sai Speaks Volume 1 Chapter 16

There is no one who can change My course or affect My conduct to the slightest extent. I am the Master over all.

- Sathya Sai Speaks Volume 1 Chapter 30

> *Every step in the career of the Avatar is pre-determined.*
> - Divine Discourse, November 23, 1968

> *The Lord will never deviate from the word.*
> - Sathya Sai Speaks Volume 2 Chapter 22

> *My activities and movements will never be altered, whatever one may say about them.*
> - Sathya Sai Speaks Volume 5 Chapter 42

> *Owing to the compulsion of circumstances some changes may take place. They are not permanent. I will not change my course because of such happenings.*
> - Sathya Sai Speaks Volume 17 Chapter 14

All of the above statements speak for themselves. To me, the most peculiar and emphatic statement of all is *"Once My Word goes forth, it must happen accordingly"*. Note that He did not stop short by merely stating that He knew whatever was going to happen. That would have been a given. He went beyond that and proclaimed: **whatever comes out, comes about**!

Change of plan? Only to the naysayers, I say!

So what is His plan?

> *The Lord alone is aware of the Plan, for His is the Plan. You see only a part of the play on the stage and so it is all very confused. When the entire story is unfolded, then you will appreciate His Plan, not until then.*
> - Sathya Sai Speaks Volume 1 Chapter 30

CHAPTER 2: What is His plan?

No one can anticipate or predict what His plans are. Swami has mentioned many times that we should all love His uncertainty. The only thing that is certain is that whatever He has said is bound to happen. How? When? Where?...the answers are beyond us mortals. Only time shall unfold the mystery.

Love my uncertainty! For it is not a mistake. It is My Intent and Will. Remember, nothing happens without My Will. Be still. Do not want to understand; do not ask to understand. Relinquish understanding. Relinquish the imperative that demands understanding.

- Sathyam Sivam Sundaram Part 3

CHAPTER 3:
Swami talks about His lifetime on earth

On several occasions Swami has talked about His lifespan on earth. Some of them were public declarations (in discourses) whereas some others were during private interviews that were later revealed in books written by devotee(s) present during the interview. The compilation below includes some of the documented quotes from Swami's discourses and books.

1. *I will be in this mortal human form 59 years more and I shall certainly achieve the purpose of this Avathaar; do not doubt it.*

   - Divine Discourse, Prasanthi Nilayam, September 29, 1960

   [According to the above quote, Swami would live till the age of 93 or 94 years. 59 years more from 1960 would be the year 2019. In 2019, Swami's age will be 93. After His birthday on November 23 2019, He will be 94]

2. *I shall be in this body for 58 years more; I have assured you of this already.*

   - Divine Discourse, Prasanthi Nilayam, October 21, 1961

   [Points to the same age as Quote 1]

3. *Not only today, till 96 years I will be like this.*

   - Sathya Sai Speaks Volume 36 Chapter 14

4. *[Prof. Kasturi:] Baba has assured us that He will remain in the human frame beyond the year 2020.*
   - The Life of Bhagavan Sri Sathya Sai Baba, N.Kasturi, Page 235

   [In the year 2020 Swami would be 94 years old. After His birthday on November 23rd, He will be 95 years old. Since Prof. Kasturi mentions "beyond the year 2020", we can assume that this points to an age beyond 95 and can be considered as matching with quote 3]

5. *GUEST[1]: Then Prema Sai will not have much work to do! Swami will have made the world peaceful.*
   SAI: That is some 40 years away. At that time the world will be peaceful. That is the Name: Prema Sai. All will be love -- love, love, love everywhere.
   -My Baba and I, J.S.Hislop, Page 189.
   From an Interview in December 1978

   [The above conversation does not give conclusive evidence as to when Swami would leave His body. However it gives a clue that Prema Sai Avatar will be beyond 2018 and that Sathya Sai Avatar would already have made the world peaceful by then. Again this matches with quote 3]

6. *One odd item emerged from this interview. Baba told us that He would live to be 94 years of age.*
   - Modern Miracles, Erlendur Haraldsson, Page 46

7. *One of Baba's predictions I will leave with readers to check in due time; He has frequently repeated that He will live to be 94 years of age.*
   -Modern Miracles, Erlendur Haraldsson, Page 294

---

[1] A devotee in the interview room along with Dr.Hislop.

8. *This body will live to age 96 and will remain young.*
   - Conversations with Sathya Sai Baba, by J.S.Hislop, Birth Day Publishing Co., San Diego, CA, 1978, Page 83 (mentioned interview is published only in this edition).

9. *His (Swami's) college students had the privilege to see another unique creation in the Ootacamund Summer Course in **June 1976**. Svami, who declared that **He would live to see ninety six years in this body**, mentioned that eighteen important institutions would be established by Him all over India **in the remaining forty six years** [...]*
   - Baba: Satya Sai Part 2, Ra.Ganapati, Page 85

[According to the above quote, Swami would live 46 years after June 1976. This indicates a date in 2022 (or even late 2021)]

While Swami's age has been mentioned as 94 in some of the quotes above, on few other occasions Swami has mentioned 96 years (for His disappearance from earth). Some prophecies about Sathya Sai Avatar also mention the age of 96.

Let us try to analyze the quotes above to determine Swami's predicted time of leaving this earth.

   a. Quotes 1 and 2 point to a time frame between October 2019 and August 2020.
   b. Quotes 3 and 8 would mean that Swami would leave His body any time between December 2021 to November 2022.
   c. Quotes 4 and 5 could be considered as matching quotes 3 and 8.

CHAPTER 3: Swami talks about His lifetime on earth   37

   d. Quotes 6 and 7 indicate a time period from December 2019 to November 2020.
   e. Quote 9 indicates a date in the year 2022 (or even late 2021) that can be considered as inclusive in quotes 3 and 8.

If we just take the analysis "a" and "d" where age 94 is mentioned and correlate them, we would get a time period of December 2019 to August 2020. Comparing this to analysis "b" (considering "c" and "e" as matching "b") above which refers to 96 years, we can see a discrepancy in the range of 15 months to 36 months. In other words, between the two different versions about Swami's lifespan, one where He mentions 94 and another where He mentions 96, there is a difference of at least 15 months.

[The minimum difference calculated as between and excluding August 2020 and December 2021 which comes to 15 months. The maximum difference calculated as between and inclusive of December 2019 and November 2022 which comes to 36 months.]

One possible explanation

I never utter a word that does not have significance.
- The Life of Bhagavan Sri Sathya Sai Baba, N.Kasturi, Page 196

Is there an explanation for the above discrepancy between Swami's two different statements? We can only speculate since He alone knows what it means. The only thing we know for sure is that He does not make mistakes. Whatever Swami says has to take place. Looking from that angle, we can try to deduce a conclusion.

On one hand Swami says He will be in His body for 94 years and at another time He indicates that He will be around for 96 years. So what does that mean? **Was it a hint that Swami will be "out of" His body[1] for around two years?** It could very well be a possibility. Well, He is "out of" His body right now[2], is He not?

If we apply the "period of discrepancy" determined from my earlier analysis, it could mean that **Swami may "return" after 15 months and before 36 months** of His leaving the body. Since Swami left His body on April 24, 2011, this period could be between **July 2012 and April 2014**.

Trust in My wisdom. I do not make mistakes.
- Sanathana Sarathi August 1984

---

[1] Or disappear.
[2] As of April 8, 2012, the date of publishing the first edition.

CHAPTER 4:
Sai predictions for the future

Swami has said many things about Himself and His mission. As we know, many of Swami's predictions have already come to pass. But some of them are to happen in the near future or has only partially occurred yet. I have made a humble attempt to collect and list a few here. (Please note that these are provided here only to establish the certainty of more wonderful times to come in the Sathya Sai Avatar).

> *I will have to forego the car and even the aeroplane when I move from place to place, for the crowds pressing around them will be too huge;* ***I will have to move across the sky; yes, that too will happen, believe Me.***
>
> *- Sathya Sai Speaks Volume 2 Chapter 18*

> *Believe Me, a day will come, when you will barely be able to spot a tiny red flash of My robes, from a long distance, that too with a great effort.* ***You will realize Swami's glory when I walk across the sky from one end to the other.***
>
> *- Thapovanam Sri Sathya Sai Sathcharithra, Jandhyala Venkateswara Sastry, Chapter 11*

> *Formerly when the Govardhanagiri was raised aloft by the little boy, the gopees and gopaalas realised that Krishna was the Lord.* ***Now, it is not one Govardhanagiri, a whole range will be lifted, you will see! Have patience, have faith.***
>
> *- Sathya Sai Speaks Volume 3 Chapter 15*

[In this case Swami could have been using a metaphor to explain the enormity of His task. But with Swami anything is possible]

*Again how fortunate you are that **you can witness all the countries of the world paying homage to Bharatha; you can hear adoration to Sathya Sai's Name reverberating throughout the world, even while this body is existing, before you. And again, you can witness very soon the restoration of Sanathana Dharma to its genuine and natural status**, the Dharma laid down in the Vedas for the good of all the peoples of the world.*
- Divine Discourse, May 17, 1968

*This body has been assumed, to serve a purpose: **the establishment of Dharma** and the teaching of Dharma. **When that purpose is over, this Body will disappear**, like the bubble on the waters.*
- Sathya Sai Speaks Volume 10 Chapter 39

As is evident from the quotes above, Swami clearly talks about the wonderful miracles to come while He would still be in the current form. Swami also talks about how all the countries would pay homage to India while His body would still exist. He also mentions about the complete establishment of *Dharma* before His body would disappear.

While Swami's statements mentioned above clearly indicate the events to come during His lifetime, Swami has also given indications of many more wonderful things to come during the Sathya Sai Avatar. The excerpts provided below are derived from Swami's discourses and documented interviews. The original quotations are provided in a further chapter *"Dawning of the Sathya Sai Golden Age"*.

- The world will already be peaceful when Prema Sai arrives.
- Swami will usher in a Golden Age that will come sooner than everyone expects. No one can imagine the beauty of that Golden Age. It will be magnificent beyond all dreams.
- The change will be universal and occur in every place.
- Sai *Rashtra* (Nation) will be established and blessed indeed are those who will be able to experience that Heaven on earth.
- All the unrest will soon be eradicated from the face of earth. Everyone will develop sacred feelings. All will enjoy the divine bliss. The entire nation will enjoy peace and happiness soon. There will not be any difficulties or suffering.
- People of all the countries will be united.
- Swami's name and form will soon be found getting established everywhere. They will occupy every inch of the world.
- In Sai gatherings there won't be place for people to stand even.
- Sai Organization membership will be of great advantage in the future. Sai gatherings will attract so many people that it may not be possible to accommodate the general public. All available spaces may be assigned to people within the Sai Organization.
- The whole world will be transformed into Sathya Sai Organization and Sathya Sai will be installed in the hearts of one and all.
- All countries will pay homage to India. India will be the leader of the world in all respects - spiritually,

culturally, socially, politically and economically.
- In the days ahead the whole world will be obliged to come to Prasanthi Nilayam.
- We will all witness Puttaparthi becoming a Madhura Nagara (birth place of Krishna). Everywhere world maps are going to mark Puttaparthi as an important location.

[Please refer to Chapter 9 *"Dawning of the Sathya Sai Golden Age"* for original quotations.]

We have no business to doubt

Prof.Kasturi explains in *Sathyam Shivam Sundaram* (Part 4) how the small hamlet called Puttaparthi which Arnold Schulman once described as "scarce five minutes from the Stone Age" was transformed into a beautiful spiritual heaven by the Divine Will alone. When Swami was only seventeen, He confided to one of the priests named Lakshmiah that people would come in huge numbers to Puttaparthi for His *Darshan*. Lakshmiah could not believe what he had heard because such a thing did not seem possible at that time. As years passed by and crowds started to gather in huge numbers, Lakshmiah had to be content catching a glimpse of the Lord from far away. By then he did believe!

Swami declared on His 65th birthday that He would build a state-of-the-art super specialty hospital to provide free medical care and that it would be ready for the first heart operation in only one year. Experts scoffed at and said it could not be done. Some of Bhagawan's own staff questioned where the funds would come from to sustain such a mammoth endeavor. Dr Keith Critchlow, eminent architect who designed the Hospital also had his own doubts. "Even in a very technically advanced country like the USA, a super speciality hospital of this kind cannot be constructed in less than seven years. How then can Swami build this hospital in six months?" he wondered[1]. Contrary to all doubts, in accordance with the Divine Will, the Hospital was inaugurated the very next year on the occasion of His 66th birthday and as many as four open heart surgeries were performed! Even after listening to many such stories of miraculous transpirations, we still tend to entertain doubts. In fact, the state of matters would scoop to such levels as to force the Lord Himself clarify His assertions as not being tall or exaggerated.

Embodiments of Divine Love! Do not regard what I am going to say as an exaggeration. There is not a trace of self-interest in Me.

- Sathya Sai Speaks Volume 23 Chapter 34

The Sai Saga has shown us that things which were once perceived incomprehensible would later manifest miraculously as an epitome of His Divine Will. People who had doubted would later hail those very same things as only incidental to His Mission; being conferred as a glimpse of His Glory. Most of them forget that they once had their own suspicions about the plausibility of such things. Those who remember become ashamed and repent of their ignorance in doubting the Avatar.

When Swami says something will happen, it is bound to happen. We have no business to doubt it. Let us pray to Him to grant us the wisdom and discernment to assimilate the certitude of such marvelous things that are destined to transpire with the omnipotence of Sri Sathya Sai Avatar, even as we collectively contemplate on the majesty of His Glory!

---

[1]Reference: Thapovanam Sri Sathya Sai Sathcharithra by Jandhyala Venkateswara Sastry.

PART 2

The New Coming

CHAPTER 5:
Clues for His imminent return

Swami has declared that there will be a new era of love and peace on this earth which He called the "*Golden Age*" that is to come during His lifetime.

> *Many hesitate to believe that things will improve, that life will be happy for all and full of joy, and that **the golden age will recur. Let me assure you that this Dharmaswarupa, that this Divine body, has not come in vain.** It will succeed in averting the crisis that has come upon humanity.*
> - Baba in 1968 - Sai Baba, The Holy Man and the Psychiatrist, Page 91

[Please see the chapter "*Dawning of the Sathya Sai Golden Age*" for more quotes from Swami on the ensuing Golden Age]

Swami has talked in length about the Golden Age during many discourses and interviews. He has also revealed some astonishing details about the ensuing Golden Age to some of His close devotees. A British Sai devotee Lucas Ralli has compiled some of Swami's messages in the book *"Sai Messages for You and Me"* that has been published in four volumes. One of the messages says:

> *The arrival of the Golden Age shall be heralded **by a new coming** as well as some upheavals, sufficient to uproot the evil that is so prevalent today.*
> - Sai Messages for You and Me Vol.II, Ralli, Lucas, 1988, Page 70

Until now all the different books I have seen that refers to the above statement have interpreted the "new coming" as the coming of Prema Sai Baba. But with Swami leaving His body earlier than expected, the above statement takes a new meaning. Was Swami giving a hint about His "new coming" in the very same form as Sathya Sai Baba? Especially since He mentions that the Golden Age would come during the Sathya Sai Avatar itself? In this age of rampant evil and disharmony, in my opinion, only a miracle of such magnanimous proportion can uproot the evil and turn the attention of people towards God.

Prof. V.K. Gokak was an eminent Indian poet, professor and the first Vice-Chancellor of the Sri Sathya Sai Institute of Higher Learning. He had received many a personal audience with Swami and written several books about Him. In his book *"Bhagavan Sri Sathya Sai Baba"*, he suggests that there will be a defining moment in the career of Sathya Sai Avatar that he calls the "Hour of God"(Page 54). Could that defining moment be the coming back of Sathya Sai form? Swami has also indicated that the Golden Age will be triggered by an event (or series of events) that will draw world attention to His Divinity.

> **The day of awakening** *is not far away and when it comes* **there will be a revelation of the true power of God***, a manifestation of the omnipresence of the Lord. This will be the signal of a great move forward and the weeding out of those who are not ready to accept the challenge of the moment.*
>
> - Sai Messages for You and Me Vol.I,
> Ralli, Lucas, 1985

A miracle to come

Before He left His body on April 24, 2011, Bhagawan granted three inspirational messages to Seema Dewan, a devotee who lives in Canton, Ohio, USA. Seema Dewan is a familiar name to many devotees because her books are famous throughout the Sai Community. In August of 1990 Swami had asked Seema Dewan to record all her inner conversations with Him because they would benefit mankind one day. That is how she started writing her first book *"Sai Darshan"* (Published by Sri Sathya Sai Publications Trust of Prasanthi Nilayam). During the month of September 1997, Swami blessed the manuscript of the book during the *Darshan* eleven times and twice poured *vibhuthi* on it. Just like her book "Sai Darshan", those messages that Swami granted to her (through visions and inner conversations) just before He passed away has been an immense source of solace and inspiration to many Sai devotees all over the world. In her own words[1]:

> *He (Swami) told me at that point that these three messages, "For Your Sake Only", "Everything is Possible", and "A Miracle to Come" would be the last regarding His health, and that they* **would always be a comforting tool in the hands of His devotees***. He also instructed me to ask Ted and Jody Henry[2] to make a video of His third message.*

---

[1]All excerpts of messages received by Seema Dewan are taken from saidivineinspirations.blogspot.com.

[2]Ted Henry is a retired television journalist and long time Sai devotee from Cleveland, Ohio. He, along with his wife Jody has conducted many video interviews with Sai devotees. These videos are available in their website souljourns.net. Video versions of the messages received by Seema Dewan are also available in their website.

The message "A Miracle to Come" was received by Seema Dewan on April 23, 2011, a day before Swami left His body. In that message Swami says (excerpts only provided):

> *A miracle is to come My dears...I alone know it best. If you can wait for the days to pass and keep yourself in fortitude, if you can just hold on...a little more than you think you can, then you My dears are about to see that which I shall unfold for you to witness...For you to live...A miracle is to come. You have prayed for it.*

About the message Seema Dewan says (excerpts only provided):

> *He then came to me Saturday morning with the message, "A Miracle...to Come". He gave it to me early in the morning but did not allow me to share it until 9 am. He promised me there was a Golden Era yet to come.* ***Of course, I thought at that point that He will re-enter the body. Swami never explains things clearly but makes sure His work gets done.***

As Seema Dewan herself acknowledges, at that time she had thought Swami would cure Himself and return. Anyone who read the message at that time would have thought the same since Swami mentions that a miracle was to come. Yet He left His body next day. What then was the miracle Swami was referring to?

Swami gave her another message, a day after He left His body (on April 25, 2011): *"I Have Gone Nowhere"* (excerpts only provided).

CHAPTER 5: Clues for His imminent return

> [...]*The devoted hearts with a pure mind and a loving heart shall call Me from time to time. They alone with the strength of their purity* **shall make Me once again visible to the world and I will come once again with My hands full***. You must believe in My word for whatever I say never goes to waste. Whatever I say becomes truth. Always remember Me, know that I am before you.* **Free yourself from emotion and await My return***.*

In this message Swami states that He would be visible to this world once again. It could be interpreted as the coming of Prema Sai Baba. But why then would He use the expression "visible to the world" to describe His return? (We will discuss more on this in a further chapter *"A Vision in the Sky?"*). Only if we read this message in conjunction with the previous one (*"A Miracle to Come"*), we get an indication of the impending miracle. The miracle He was talking about cannot be the arrival of Prema Sai Baba since that is already being expected and awaited upon. For the same reason, the assurances of *"You must believe in My word for whatever I say never goes to waste"* and *"Whatever I say becomes truth"* cannot be ascribed to the coming of Prema Sai Baba as well. It was the form of Sathya Sai Avatar that "left" earlier than expected. Hence the assurance, a timely one at that, should have been pertaining to the return of the same form of Sathya Sai Baba. However, since Swami asks to *"hold on a little more than you think you can"*, the prospect of His immediate return can be ruled out. And this corroborates the many other clues that are presented in this book on His imminent return[1].

---

[1] These interpretations are of the author.

Dreams of devotees

A dream from Swami can happen only by His Will. It is real and conveys a clear message to the concerned devotee.

> *Swami appearing in dreams is very auspicious [...] Dreams are reflection, reaction and resound of that which is within you. The same does not apply to the dream in which Swami appears. Swami appears in dreams only when He Wills it, and not when you want them.*
> - Sathya Sai Speaks Volume 31 Chapter 44

> *Dreams which are Willed by Me are very clear and give you no room for confusion or doubt. I come to you and convey what I want to, in the most direct manner.*
> - Sathya Sai Speaks Volume 31 Chapter 44

A few months after Swami left His body, Sri B.N. Narasimhamurthi[1] had a dream in which Swami gives him detailed instructions concerning the Muddenhalli campus (of Sri Sathya Sai Institute of Higher Learning) where he is currently serving as the warden.

Swami says in the dream[2] (excerpts only provided):

> *Get the hill-top building ready for my stay before I arrive on this GuruPurnima day (15th July, 2011). On GuruPurnima day I will enter there and stay there permanently. I will go from here to different*

---

[1] Author of "Sathyam Sivam Sundaram", the official biography of Sri Sathya Sai Baba (volumes 5 & 6).

[2] Excerpts are from www.ssso.net.

CHAPTER 5: Clues for His imminent return

> places and come back. But I will stay here permanently.

Swami goes on to mention that He will also be visible there.

> Swami then said "Nenu akkadiki vastaanu, akkada kanabadutaanu". (I will come there and also I will be seen there).

On the above statement of Swami in his dream, Sri Narasimhamurthi elaborates:

> To whom He will be visible and to whom not is left to His sweet will. There was a time when He granted wholesale Darshan whether anyone deserved or not. That opportunity came to a close on 24th April 2011. **Those of us who deserve His Darshan will get it - can see Him physically also when He wills.** Because, in my association with Him for past 46 or so years, none of His words have gone untrue. I am very very sure we will see Him one day or the other.

Late Dr.K.Hanumanthappa, former vice-chancellor of Sri Sathya Sai University has described in detail in his book "*Sri Sathya Sai Baba A Yugavatar*" about his dream where Swami shows him the future of Puttaparthi. In chapter "*Future Vision of Puttaparthi*", Dr.K.Hanumanthappa explains (pages 165-167):

> One day, in my dream, Swamy started explaining how Puttaparthi will be in future. He took me to an elevated place, and from there He started showing one by one, the most important developments. Among many significant things that I saw were Swamy having shifted His stay from the present

> *Prashanthi Mandir to a palatial building on the Hill opposite to Chitravathi River. A big compound wall was being built surrounding the Hill [...] The entire compound is protected by the military with arms.*

Some relevant points from the dream:

- Devotees from different countries have built colonies around Puttparthi. Swami would come down the hill and split Himself into multiple forms and would go simultaneously to these colonies for giving *Darshan*.
- Swami would multiply Himself into hundreds of Babas and go to each center in each country to give *Darshan*.
- Puttaparthi has grown to a very vibrant and flourishing city, so big like the New York City with ultra modern facilities.
- Only few selected devotees have access to meet Swami.
- Even to have a glimpse of Swami would become very difficult for devotees in the future.

Dr.K.Hanumanthappa was a distinguished scholar and has had so many wonderful experiences with Swami. In the mentioned book, he has explained how Swami guided him through dreams in various instances of his life. In fact, Swami Himself confirms the authenticity of those dreams (page 8). It is also interesting to note that this book was released by Swami Himself on March 7, 2008 - Mahashivarathri day. In the event of Swami's return, all these future visions would beautifully fall into place. Before Swami's departure from the physical, Sai devotees could easily envision such happenings in the future but now would it be appropriate to regard these dreams as mere fantasies? Swami's dreams are not stretches of devotee's imagination as He Himself asserts:

CHAPTER 5: Clues for His imminent return

> *When I appear in a dream, it is to communicate something to the individual. It is not a mere dream as is generally known.* ***Do not think that these incidents you experience in your dream as stretches of your imagination.***
> - Sathyam Sivam Sundaram Part 4, Page 100

With Swami's Grace, I have been fortunate enough to listen to the experiences of many Sai devotees who share similar belief as I do about Swami's return. While some of them do not believe that Swami would stay on as before, they all think that there could be large scale miracles and His "appearances" or "visions" to masses in multiple parts of the world. Few devotees even had dreams about Swami's reemergence.

One of the most revealing dreams about Swami's return that I have come across is that of Sri Jairo Borjas. Jairo is from Venezuela and has been a Sai Devotee since 1988. He has been an active devotee in Orlando, Colombia, Mexico and Venezuelan Sai Centers holding different positions in the Sai Organization. He has traveled to the Prasanthi Nilayam several times. In 1997-1998 he stayed in the Ashram for a year as instructed by Swami Himself in interviews. Nowadays he lives in Bogota, Colombia.

On April 29, 2012 he had a beautiful dream in which Swami instructs him to spread the word among fellow Sai devotees that an exceptional moment in the history of mankind is drawing close! Following is an excerpt of the translated version of his original narration in Spanish[1]:

---

[1]Published here with permission from Sri Jairo Borjas. His original narration in Spanish was translated with the help of Sri Ana Diaz-Viana, a common friend to Jairo and the author.

Last night, before arriving home, I began to feel Swami's voice telling me to prepare for what is about to happen. The voice kept asking me "Are you ready?", "Are you ready?" Then it became stronger and stronger that initially scared me. I did not want to get home because I did not know how to answer the question. So I started chanting the *Gayatri mantra*, while telling Swami that I as His son was worthy of all His love and protection and I was always prepared for Him and that my faith in Him as my loving Father and God would always protect me. But the voice was still getting stronger and then I became convinced that it was meant to prepare me for something great and extraordinary.

After I got home, I started working as I usually do before going to sleep. Being so tired I could not continue much longer and soon fell asleep chanting *Gayatri*. Swami came to me in such a vivid dream. In the dream I was with my students of Sai Spiritual Education, one of them named Narada who Swami mentioned was actually a descendant of the great Sage. Then Swami approached us waving His hand, looked extremely beautiful and young. He gave us *Padnamaskar*, (touching the Lotus Feet of the Lord) amazingly it was an experience of such depth that I felt He was right there for real. So real that I could swear I experienced His physical body. Swami told me that He was indeed alive and that He had not left His body. Tears of joy flowed from my eyes as He touched and embraced me.

Swami then took my hand and led me to the interview room. After we got inside He asked me

CHAPTER 5: Clues for His imminent return

Are you ready? And said: "It is time and I need you. Be willing to do what I say". I was in such a state of ecstasy that I had never experienced before, something that surpasses anything describable. I told Swami, "My body is your body, my mind is your mind, I surrender to you". Extending my arms I told Him that they were His arms and so was my body that He could use as He liked. I pleaded to Him that I should never be out of that state of consciousness, where I knew no difference between my Swami and I. I did not wish to get back to sleep without being permanently conscious of that reality, keeping that state of fulfillment and bliss. He told me: "*I need you dear son to do some things for me*". So I said yes and only asked Him to give me clarity on what His Will was. To that He presented me a smile that filled me with such radiant light that had invaded all my being till then.

Afterwards, He took me to the Shrine of my sister Coro...there was a carpet where Coro meditates... Entering there, Swami became Lord Rama Himself and told me that the place was full of name of God and the love of God. He told me that Coro was a great devotee, always reciting His name and thinking of Him. Moving around the altar, then He began to dance a sort of *Tandava* dance in ecstasy, tears of joy streaming down His eyes, and flashed in a shining light spilling bliss. Telling me: "The name of Lord Rama pervades everything here, Coro is a great devotee, and she is very loved and cherished". In that state of joy at the end of the dance He transformed back into Baba and said I am God, moreover I am all names and forms.

We were back in the interview room. Baba explained that pure-hearted devotees make the Divinity manifest when the Divine name is recited, and Coro, is a devotee centered in God, reciting His name. With tears of joy in His eyes, saying this kind of devotion touches me...He told me that's what all devotees should do. **Then very emphatically He told me that we are about to witness an exceptional moment in the history of mankind, it will be very soon, and that His power and glory will manifest in ways we had never seen or even imagined.** That time is drawing close....

Swami told me: *"My devotees should awaken from the dream. I am not the body, or one form of God or the other, but all the names and all forms. How can that eternal and immeasurable God be limited to one shape? How can it be said that I attained a state of bliss or that I am in Samadhi or Mahasamadhi, when I as God am always in bliss and in fact I am bliss Myself? If I am what you have always been looking for, I am the source itself of all happiness and bliss"*.

"Oh devotees, wake up, wake up, wake up... the time for which great Sages and Sidhas have been waiting for eons...is fast approaching. Realize who I am, my reality of that Omnipresence, that Greatness; and Majesty and prepare yourself for an extraordinary event that is about to unfold....IN WHICH I WILL RETURN IN WAYS THAT YOU CAN NEVER IMAGINE. Trust me, have complete faith and surrender. Very soon all will realize my glory and greatness".

"Now you go around the world and spread my message. Tell all to be prepared. This is a great time and a great opportunity, something extraordinary in the history of mankind is about to happen". Swami ended His words and bid me goodbye; I listened with my eyes full of tears and begged Him not to go, not to let me back into this world of illusion. I pleaded Him to keep my mind on the eternal and take care of the mundane things, as my hands would always be used for serving Him. Oh Swami, you are always the doer, let me live in this happiness and bliss forever. Shaking His hand I said goodbye. I was bathed in tears of love, joy and ecstasy. Oh my dear Lord how much I love you!

The dream of Jairo Borjas gives clear indication of a wonderful event to come. Many Sai devotees have shared with me the details of their dreams in which Swami clearly indicates His imminent reappearance. However, since such dreams are of a personal or one-to-one nature between Swami and His devotee, the details are better left unpublished. To provide a gist, those dreams are clear indications to the concerned devotees that Swami will be back in the same physical form. Some devotees also had astonishingly identical dreams about Swami appearing in various places simultaneously with many people around the world claiming to have seen the vision. I came across excitingly similar prophecies mentioned in some scriptures, the details of which are provided in subsequent chapters.

Only time will tell what Swami has in store for all of us. But from the dreams and experiences of various Sai devotees, I am convinced that we are in for something spectacular.

CHAPTER 6:
Incredible Nadis

Nadis are sacred palm leaf texts written by Sages of India thousands of years ago. They are mostly written in the ancient Tamil language in the form of poetic verses. The Sages recorded these predictions for every individual for the betterment of humanity and to safeguard *dharma* (righteousness). These Sages predicted the characteristics, family history, spiritual life as well as the careers of innumerable individuals. *"Nadi"* in Tamil language means "in search of". This is because the scriptures contain some unique predictions of specific natives, who would come seeking them at a particular stage of their lifetime as foretold by the great Saints. The *Rishis* (Sages) who dictated those Nadis were gifted with such remarkable foresight that they accurately foretold the entire future of mankind. Many scholars in different parts of India have in their safekeeping several *Nadi granthas* (palm leaf books). Some of these palm leaf inscriptions available in Tamilnadu (in South India) were standardized, ordered and classified nearly 1000 years ago during the reign of Chola Kingdom. There are a number of Nadis available (that are named after the *Rishis* or Saints who composed them) like *Agasthya Nadi*, *Suka Nadi*, *Brahma Nadi*, *Kausika Nadi* etc. There are only a few Nadi readers available who can correctly interpret the inscriptions that are written in the poetic language.

Prophecies about Sathya Sai Avatar in Nadis

There was an article in *Sanathana Sarathi* of February 1961 entitled "Bhagawan Sathya Sai Baba's 500-year old Horoscope". It talks in length about Dr. E.V. Sastry, a famous and prominent member of Indian Astro-Occult Research Association in New Delhi, who found the Nadi inscriptions containing amazing details and predictions about Bhagawan Sri Sathya Sai Baba and His life that had been recorded in palm leaves hundreds of years ago. Shakuntala Balu, in her book *"Living Divinity"*, records the readings from *Suka Nadi* that is in possession of a well-known astrology professor in Bangalore, Sri Ganjur Narayana Shastry. All these Nadi readings describe accurately and at great length, Sri Sathya Sai Baba's family tree and many facts about him. Many Sai devotees have confirmed and written about Nadi readings that reveal the splendor of Sai Avatar and the various miracles and extraordinary deeds that He would perform[1].

Some of the characteristics of Sathya Sai Avatar mentioned in Nadis:

Brahma Nadi:

- The Avatar creating an illusion as though He is a human being, a denizen of Parthi (Puttaparthi), Sathya Sai Narayana (Sai Baba's original name), the incarnation of Shakti-Shiva, the incarnation of Shirdi Baba (His previous incarnation), peace in person in the peaceful precincts of Parthi on the banks of the river Chithravati.
- Reincarnation of Sri Krishna, Sri Linga, Sri Rudra Kali, Sri Shakti, Sri Vishnu.
- An embodiment of truth in the garb of a human, living as Avatar in Maharashtra at Shirdi as Shirdi

---

[1] References for Nadi Predictions:
    a. Living Divinity by Shakuntala Balu
    b. Sri Sathya Sai Avathar by V.Aravind Subramaniyam
    c. In Search of Sai Divine By Satya Pal Ruhela

Baba, wearing tattered clothes, with the look of poverty and a life of simplicity, taking yet another Avatar as Sathyanarayana with a serpent couch.
- Like Dattatreya, an Avatar conjoining the trinity (Brahma, Vishnu, Shiva) together.
- The supreme preceptor comes as a form of Shakti. Sathya Sai taking another avatar as Prema Sai (His next incarnation).
- The day Thursday sanctified by the boy Sathya Sai.

Agastya Nadi:

- He is the divine embodiment of grace and the father of the world.
- The Avatar Sathya Sai will be medical master of lightning efficiency.
- He will form many educational institutions, produce literature on righteous conduct and preach throughout His life on spirituality.
- He will leave home at a young age and launch upon the establishment of dharma (righteousness) as His life's mission. In the previous life, He was Sai Baba of Shirdi.

Suka Nadi:

- Through His Grace, Love and wisdom He will establish *Nithyanandha* - The everlasting bliss, in this world.
- The place where He lives will become a holy land of penance.
- He will always have pleasure and happiness by serving the mankind.
- He is an Avatar amidst the Avatars.

CHAPTER 6: Incredible Nadis

- He is a great *sankalpa siddha* (a master of will) and one of great powers, but without any attraction to worldly wealth or glory.
- He will have the power of *ichhamarana prapti* (the ability to die at will) and that He is one in the *Nirvikalpa Samadhi* state, living only for the nurturing of righteousness.
- His mission will be of relieving the distressed.
- He will be born to propagate righteousness and the place where He will live will become a holy land.
- He will be able to assume different forms and be seen in several places simultaneously and to remove difficulties and obstacles to avert danger.
- He will establish an ashram near a place where there are vehicles with many wheels (Train station. Refers to Whitefield Ashram) and will also re-establish educational institutions of spiritual strength.
- He will show omniscience in many ways to devotees who, if they surrender to Him in full faith, will be given the opportunity of shedding their sins and of finding peace and goodness.
- His glory will spread far and wide and many people will come to him. But all shall not receive His grace due to past actions.
- He is a great *brahmachari* (celibate) and will help others in establishing righteousness. His attitude towards men and women will show equality. He will be a mother among women.
- He will be an Incarnation of Love (*Premaswarupa*), Joy (*Anandaswarupa*), Wisdom (*Jnanaswarupa*), but only those who are enlightened will be able to experience Him as Joy (*Ananda*).

- He can be experienced, but not expressed; as a dumb mute can eat but not speak. Total equanimity will be His. He sees the world as a blade of grass. He will not be concerned with public opinion and will do only what is right.
- He will be a representative of Shirdi Sai Baba and will be born as a result of the prayers addressed to Shirdi Sai Baba.
- He will give *Samadhi Darshan* to Shirdi Sai Devotees; and similarly, after He has flown from this body, Sathya Sai devotees will have *Samadhi Darshan* at Whitefield, which will be venerated as sacred soil.
- His life will be for the good of mankind in the way described by Krishna in the *Bhagavad Gita*.
- He will also plant a tree in Brindavan, Bangalore, and that place will become a *siddhikshetra* (a field of energy) and the tree a *kalpavrusha* (a wish-fulfilling tree).
- Good will accrue to anyone who only sees Sri Sathya Sai Baba. His grace will make people overcome their problems, surmount difficulties and guide them towards progress.
- He will show himself in many places simultaneously, though He will actually be in one place, and there will be many divine acts and manifestations.
- He is tolerant and compassionate of nature and treats everyone equally. He does not hurt feelings or express anger when errors of ignorance are committed.
- Often He speaks in jest, but He speaks Truth. When He publicizes any aspect of himself or His activities, which is not always, He does so at particular times and it is only and always for the

growth of righteousness: instilling good ideas of life and creating an atmosphere of goodwill.
- This Avatar will have healing powers and the power to cure himself by the sprinkling of water. He will use His healing powers not only for the people of this world, but also for the beings of other worlds, and on a higher plane of existence (*Devas* or Celestial beings).
- Sainath does everything according to a plan He has.
- He has great purification powers. Merely the sight of him, or the slightest of word exchanged with him, can purify one. He also has the power to lengthen life.
- Sainatha (Lord Sai) is *Mahavishnu Swarupa*, a form of Great Vishnu himself.
- Sathya Sai Baba will always retain a youthful look, age notwithstanding.

The very incarnation of all the Divine forms into one God as Sri Sathya Sai is emphasized clearly in all these Nadis. All the exact details what we see and hear today are portrayed very clearly with each and every detail. The Suka Nadi also gave yet another interesting prophecy that this Avatar Sathya Sai Baba will mount a Golden Sun chariot (*Swarna- Aadhithya Ratham*) on an auspicious day and will be drawn in procession by the devotees. The day mentioned was of the year named *Eeshwara* (One of 60 years in Indian calendar), on Monday, *Sashti thithi* of *Krishna Paksha* (sixth day of the darker fortnight) in the month of *Bhaadra-Padha* (sixth month according to Indian calendar i.e. 15 September to 15 October). The auspicious time predicted was around 7 AM.

In the year 1997 during the *Padhuka Mahotsav* (a festival for worshipping sandals blessed by the Lord), under the leadership of Sri Subramanian Chettiar, President of Sri Sathya Sai Padhuka Trust, devotees of Madurai (in Tamilnadu) brought a golden chariot for Swami. The chariot had a golden throne crowned by a golden umbrella and a huge golden disc of the *Soorya*, the Sun God at the back. The golden idol of Shiva and Parvathi was placed in the chariot of Shiva-Shakthi Avatar. The driver for this magnificent golden chariot was the four-faced Brahma, the Creator. Exactly on the day specified i.e. on 22 September 1997 on Monday, as specified in the Nadi the historic event took place. Bhagawan came from His Divine residence, surrounded by devotees, students and Vedic scholars. With rhythmic and pleasing traditional music combined with the loud and splendid chanting of Veda, Bhagawan mounted the chariot on 7.05 AM. Swami with His amazing glory, illuminated with the golden rays of the early morning rising sun, proceeded towards the Prasanthi Mandir in the chariot.

These Nadis accurately predicted the glory and splendor of Sathya Sai Avatar thousands of years ago. Some of the prophecies in various Nadis point to a glorious time in the near future wherein Swami's powers will be revealed to the entire world and He will be regarded as the "Great Emperor".

- When the *Kali Yuga* influence grows even more intense, then people will see His true might and will acknowledge that He is the Supreme Power. Then mankind will bow to Him as to a great emperor.
- He will keep an airplane airborne for a long time after it runs out of fuel, through His will alone.
- He will erect a flag staff of righteousness at a significant time and thereafter righteousness will visibly increase.

- At present He displays only one tenth of His real self. After a while, His efforts to save the world will increase tenfold. He will show that He alone can control the fury of nature.
- Now *adharma* (unrighteousness) has grown to three fourths proportion. When it increases by one fourth more, that is when all becomes unrighteousness, Sri Sathya Sai Baba's full powers will come into play and be known in the world. Evil has to rise to its uttermost before His Divine quality can be fully realized.
- In a short time, His greatness will spread further and there will be universal worship of Sathya Sai.

My experience with Nadis

From my own personal experience, Nadi readings are very accurate and reliable provided the readings are conducted by an accomplished reader/astrologer. I had my own Nadi readings done in 1997-98 from a Nadi astrology center in South India. My readings were from the famous Agasthya Nadi written by Sage Agasthya, one of the seven *Maharishis* (Great Saints). I was wonderstruck by the accuracy of the readings that included the exact names of my parents, their occupation, details from my childhood and my whereabouts at that time. It also had various predictions about my future along with a timeline of events to happen in my life. The most relevant reading that needs mention here is about my Guru Sri Sathya Sai Baba. The reading goes:

> *You have a Guru. He has three incarnations. First incarnation was in Maharashtra State (Shirdi). Currently He is in His second which is in Andhra Pradesh. In this life He is Shiva-Shakthi Swaroopam (embodiment of Shiva-Shakthi principle). Name is*

Sri Sathya Sai Baba. His third incarnation will be in Karnataka State. In that He will assume the name of Prema Sai [...] You will get advices from your Guru in dreams.

I should mention here that there was no way the astrologer could have known that I was a Sai devotee. Many Sai devotees had gone there later on for readings and confirmed to me that their readings were accurate. In my life, till now all the predictions have happened exactly as foretold including the ones about my marriage, children, career, travels, spiritual life and much more.

Do Nadis have anything to say about Swami's disappearance and His impending return? Please read on.

Nadis predict Swami's return

A month after Swami left His body, a Sai devotee named Sri Vasantha Sai of Madurai in Tamilnadu (South India) wanted to find out what has been written in Nadis about Swami's early disappearance. She sent one of her associates to Vaideeshwarankoil, a Temple town in Tamilnadu where many Nadis are preserved. What transpired was nothing short of extraordinary. In own words of Sri Vasantha Sai:

SV (K S Venkatraman, an associate of Sri Vasantha Sai) left immediately, saw some Nadis and called me. He said that all the Nadis tell that Swami will come again[...]SV found many Nadis, which all confirmed what Swami told me in meditation: "He would return again"[...]SV went back in late July and read more of Swami's Nadis. All these Nadis reveal the same: Swami is coming.

CHAPTER 6: Incredible Nadis

Sri Vasantha Sai is an advanced soul, a Sai devotee for many years who has been having countless visions, dreams and miraculous experiences of the amazing grace of her Divine Lord Sri Sathya Sai Baba. In the spiritual realm, Sri Vasantha Sai's love and devotion to Bhagavan Sri Sathya Sai Baba has made her the epitome of "Radha Consciousness".

Sri Vasantha Sai has written numerous books about Swami and various aspects of spirituality. Her first book named *"Liberation! Here Itself! Right Now!"* was published in 1997. Earlier I mentioned how the prophecy about the Golden Sun chariot was rightly fulfilled as predicted in Nadis. It was under the leadership of Sri Subramanian Chettiar, President of Sri Sathya Sai Padhuka Trust, that the devotees of Madurai had brought the golden chariot for Swami. Bhagawan Sri Sathya Sai Baba had visited Sri Subramanian Chettiar's house at Madurai on May 7th, 1997 wherein He blessed Sri Vasantha Sai's book by autographing its manuscript. This is more than enough proof for the authenticity of her divine visions and experiences. She currently lives in her ashram *"Mukthi Nilayam"* (meaning source of liberation) near Madurai. Her ashram is a source of spiritual happiness and serves the poor and needy by providing free food, shelter, medicine and education.

The Nadi readings about Swami's reappearance were translated and compiled into a book *"Sacred Nadi Readings"*. In this book Sri Vasantha Sai explains:

> *Bhagavan Sri Sathya Sai Baba is not an ordinary Avatar. All think that He has left His body. Not only ordinary people, but also those who were close to Him think in this way. It is true that He has 'left the body'. However, it is also true that He will come again with the same form.*

Some excerpts from these Nadi readings from her book *"Sacred Nadi Readings"*[1] are given below:

At the time of seeing this Nadi, His body is no longer here. Yet, there is some confusion. His body is not here, yet His body is here. He will once again return and join the body, which He has prepared before He left His body. (Raja Rishi Viswamitra Nadi, Reading conducted on May 25, 2011) – Page 8

The body that performed these great deeds and the body that all have seen so far is not His real body. It is a Maya body[...]After Saturn enters Libra on the day of the full moon, the Lord will give a vision of Himself in His present form. This will be a true vision of His real body. It will be seen by many who will be filled with wonder and amazement. (Agasthya Nadi, Reading conducted on May 27, 2011) – Page 20

Though His Atma left His physical body, the same Atma will come again and attain the same physical form. This is destiny[...]He will not be in an aged body or a young body, but middle aged. (Raja Rishi Viswamitra Nadi, Reading conducted on May 31, 2011) – Page 86

[...]now at this time, her Lord is no longer in the physical body. He will come again in a new body. (Bhrigu Nadi, Reading conducted on May 31, 2011) – Page 96

---

[1] Sacred Nadi Readings – Compiled by Sri Vasantha Sai, Sri Vasantha Sai Books & Publications Trust, Mukthi Nilayam, 2011 (www.mukthinilayam.org)

CHAPTER 6: Incredible Nadis

> At the time of taking this Nadi, He is in the Atmic state[...]He has no earthly body. He will come again to earth.[...]That is His destiny.[...]At the age 88, people on earth will accept Him without doubt, blemish or shortcoming. He will live for 7 years.
> (Gorakka Nadi, Reading conducted on June 14, 2011) – Page 26

> He will then descend here, His body being the age of 58 to 60 years of age. He will be reborn on this earth in a body of this age. Only then will He reveal Himself to the world and all will know the truth.
> (Macchamuni Nadi, Reading conducted on August 5, 2011) – Page 102

Many more wondrous details are provided in these Nadis as explained in the book "*Sacred Nadi Readings*". However, each Sage has provided a different view-point about Swami's disappearance according to his own perception of the event. The predictions about the timing of Swami's expected return does not seem to be unanimous either. Some of the Nadis refer to different astrological conjunctions or celestial events after the occurrences of which, Swami is expected to reveal Himself in His "new" body. Since Nadis sometimes use cryptic language, it could be difficult to pin-point an exact time for Swami's reappearance. Suka Nadi and Raja Rishi Viswamitra Nadi mentions the age of 86 for His reappearance whereas Gorakka Nadi suggests the age of 88. Now the question is whether these age predictions are inclusive or exclusive of the years that Swami has been "out of" His body. Whatever may be the case, both 86 and 88 ages would fall in the timeframe that was suggested in the Chapter "*Swami talks about His lifetime on earth*" (that it could be between July 2012 and April 2014).

Intriguing Nostradamus Prophecy

Most of the Sai devotees are aware of the various prophecies of Nostradamus[1] pertaining to the Sathya Sai Avatar. Two of the prophecies stand out:

> *The triplicity of waters will give birth to a man*
> *Who will choose Thursday as his holy day.*
> *His voice, reign, and power will rise*
> *Across land and sea, amid storms in the East*
> — Quatrain 1:50

> *The earth and air will freeze so much water,*
> *When all will come to worship on Thursdays.*
> *What will be was never so beautiful before,*
> *From all parts of the world they will come to honor him*
> — Quatrain 10:71

It is quite evident that both of these predictions are about Sri Sathya Sai Baba. "Triplicity of waters" suggests a place surrounded by three water bodies. The Indian peninsula especially the southern part is surrounded by the Bay of Bengal, Arabian Sea and the Indian Ocean. Thursday is observed as the holy day of Bhagawan. The prophecy mentions how people from all parts of the world will come to honor the Lord.

These quatrains of Nostradamus have been a part of Sai literature wherever the "Advent of Sai" is a subject. I have come across them many a times. However, one of the

---

[1] Michel de Nostredame famously known as Nostradamus was a French seer living in the 16th century. His predictions of the future are some of the most famous in history, and continue to enjoy widespread popularity to the current day. His prophecies are in the form of four-line verses (quatrains) in groups of 100 (centuries).

CHAPTER 6: Incredible Nadis

lines in those prophecies has always intrigued me because I could not relate that to any of the events that have happened in the Sai Avatar. That line is "*The earth and air will freeze so much water when all will come to worship on Thursdays*". Nostradamus prophecies are believed to contain in the same quatrain, multiple events of significance and identifications concerning the object of prophecy. I have always suspected that it could be referring to some future event, most likely a natural phenomenon that involves water for obvious reasons. Even so, this prophecy has always remained an enigma. But only until I saw the following Nadi prophecy about Swami's return:

> *[...] On this day, wherever you look the wind and rain will come. Then Swami will come in His form in Andhra Pradesh in Prasanthi Nilayam.*
> (Kagabhujangar Nadi, Reading conducted on May 24, 2011) – Page 7

Astonishing is it not? However, beyond a certain point all prophecies and suppositions become irrelevant as Swami alone knows when and how things will pan out. What is known is that the Nadis unanimously predict Swami's return back to earth in the same form of Sri Sathya Sai Baba. Some Nadis specifically mention that His new body would be a younger or middle aged one. Let us all pray and wait for that astounding moment, one of the greatest miracles to ever happen in the history of mankind. One that could change the world for ever as we see it today!

Footnote: It might be of interest to some readers that I mention a particular prediction in my Agasthya Nadi readings (from 1997-98) which goes like this: *"You will write books about your Guru (Sri Sathya Sai Baba) and also distribute them outside (of India)".* This is indeed my first book ever; realizing a feat that I once considered to be farfetched, given my limited writing credentials. Amazingly another reading also says that I would write about the greatness of Nadis. This book fulfills that prophecy as well. O Nadis incredible!!!

CHAPTER 7:
The Disappearance of Mahdi

Who is Mahdi?

Mahdi (or Mehdi) is a messiah like figure in Islamic traditions who is believed to appear in this world before the prophesied "Judgment Day". Many Muslims believe that Allah would bring forth His messenger Mahdi at a difficult period of human history to restore the faith and establish peace in the world. Different meanings have been given for the name Mahdi which includes "guided one", "redeemer" and "promised teacher". He is sometimes referred to as Qaim or Al-Qaim (meaning "He who rises for truth") in Shia traditions. Other names that Mahdi is usually addressed with are "Al-Mahdi", "Hazrat Mahdi" and "Mahdi Moud".

Signs to identify Mahdi

Zeba Bashiruddin of Sri Sathya Sai Institute of Higher Learning, who is an ardent devotee of Sri Sathya Sai Baba has authored a revealing article "Hazrat Mehdi and Baba: Truth of a Prophecy" which was published in Sanathana Sarathi (November 1991). In it she has shown that all the prophecies about Hazrat Mahdi apply perfectly to Sri Sathya Sai Baba. According to her:

> *Muslims all over the world believe in the advent of a great leader and guide. They all know him as Mehdi(master). The prophet, Hazrat Mohammad, has indicated that Hazrat Mehdi will appear for the*

welfare of Muslims in the last decades of the fourteenth century Hijri (this century has just ended). It will be a time of trouble and materialism. The Quranic values and their practice will be ignored, and men's hearts will turn to the worship of the world and its glamour, "the other Gods" of Quranic language. The prophecy goes on to postulate that Hazrat Mehdi will restore the Truth and "Islam"[1] will be the religion of the entire world.

There are various "Hadiths" in Islamic traditions that refer to Prophet Mohammed's descriptions on the awaited Mahdi (In Islamic terminology, the term "Hadith" refers to reports of statements or actions of Mohammad). The various signs regarding the time and the person of Mahdi, more than 150 in number, were related by the holy Prophet to Hazrat Ali, the fourth Khalif and a repository of Sufi secrets. These signs became a guarded treasure of Imams, descendants of Hazrat Ali and formed a part of the Shia tradition (mainly of Iran) of the Prophetic sayings. In the 17th century A.D. the well known scholar, Md.Baqir bin Md. Taqi-Al Majlisi-Al Isfahani (1627-1698) collected them in his voluminous book, Bihar-ul-Anwar, written in Arabic.

A few of these selected sayings of the Prophet of Islam are listed here from the Persian (An Iranian language) translation of Bihar-ul-Anwar: Many Mohammedans will not know about his advent for a long time. That Holy Spirit will wear two garments, one inner and the other outer (p.239). The robe, orange in color, will be of such a shape that the contours of his back will be seen clearly (p.292, 777). His dress orange in color, will spread Light among the people (p.245). His hair, thick and dark, will

---

[1] Literal meaning of "Islam" being peace, it could be interpreted as prevalence of peace in the entire world.

CHAPTER 7: The Disappearance of Mahdi

reach His shoulders (p.25). His eyebrows are joined in the centre (p.242). His other features are: Broad and clear forehead (p.263). Straight nose with a dip in the beginning, a mole on the cheek, reminding of Hazrat Mosa, bright as a star, teeth with partings in the two front ones (p.243), Black eyes (p.777). Average height, compared with the Jewish height (p.239). The color of the face is described variously as shining like a gold-bronze coin; so bright that it is impossible to recognize the real color (p.263-293).The general impression: full of compassion, dignified, exalted (p.239).

His attitude to everyone will be brotherly, as if He knows them well (p.314). He will love all Prophets and Saints; and whatever He wants will be done. He will overcome all opposition (p.242). His devotees will find protection (p.342). People will find Him heavenly bliss personified (p.341). He will be a shelter for the helpless and the rejected (p.235). He will distribute A'be-e-Tuhur Kausr (spirituality) to people in the morning and evening (p.343) (The reference is to Baba's daily *Darshans*). Divine light will be manifested from Him (p.252). He will not bring new religion (p.6) (Baba has stressed often that He is not preaching a new religion). All knowledge and essence of all religions will blossom in His heart like a new garden (p.238). He will fill the earth with peace. He will be a friend and an adviser (p.287). He will show the Straight path (p.352). O ye Muslims, know this that He whose birth is hidden from you is your Master, HE IS MEHDI (p.292)[1].

---

[1] References:
   a. In Search of Sai Divine by Satya Pal Ruhela, M.D. Publications Pvt. Ltd, 1996.
   b. God Descends on Earth by Sanjay Kant, Sri Sathya Sai Towers Pvt. Ltd.

Other signs that are given in the book Bihar-ul-Anwar: He will give gifts that are light in weight. He will go around among his devotees and touch their heads with his hand. Every eye that sees him will be happy, not only humans but disembodied souls. **He will live 95 years.** In the last twenty years of His life, He will be the "King of the whole world" but at that time only two thirds of the world will believe Him. Muslims will recognize him **only nine years before His passing from the world.** He will make the world light and full of peace. So as not to be deceived, you should know that the Master of the world will bring things out of His body, through His mouth (reference to Shiva-lingam emergence from Swami's mouth during Shivaratri?).

In his book *"The Heart of Sai"*, R. Lowenberg says that he met in the ashram, an Iranian lady devotee known in Sai circles as "Irani ma" (meaning mother from Iran), who had found the prophecies of Prophet Muhammad (in Bihar-ul-Anwar) about the coming of the great Teacher. She explained to Lowenberg many identifying signs that coincided with the characteristics of Sri Sathya Sai Baba. Swami Maheshwaranand in his book *"Sai Baba and Nara Narayana Gufa Ashram"* mentions that even though Irani ma wanted to publish those prophecies of Prophet Mohammed in the form of a book, Swami did not give permission to do so.

A multitude of Iranian devotees flocking to Prasanthi Nilayam is in itself a testimony to the authenticity of predictions in Bihar-ul-Anwar and their convergence on the personality, characteristics and mission of the Sathya Sai Avatar. All the signs that Prophet Mohammed gives to identify Mahdi, perfectly aligns with Swami's physical features and characteristics. Similar to the Nadi prediction that *"mankind will bow to Him as to a great*

CHAPTER 7: The Disappearance of Mahdi 79

emperor", the prophecies about Mahdi mentions that He will be the *"King of the whole world"*.

Mahdi's reign on earth

Two of the prophecies in Bihar-ul-Anwar stand out for their bearing on the perception of Mahdi's incumbency on earth. One that says Mahdi **will live 95 years.** Another one that mentions Muslims would recognize him **only nine years before his passing from the world.** Assuming that the 95 years are of the Islamic Calendar[1], this would still be between 93 and 94 standard calendar years which is consistent with Swami's own statements about His lifespan (please refer to Chapter *"Swami talks about His lifetime on earth"*). The second prediction suggests an occurrence of something substantial that would make people believe in Mahdi 9 years before His eventual passing from world. Swami left His body at the age of 85. If we add 9 (or 8.75 standard years calculating from Islamic calendar) to that age it would be 94. In Chapter *"Swami talks about His lifetime on earth"*, I had already suggested that since Swami mentions the age of 94 and 96 in different places, the two years of discrepancy could account to the number of years He will be "out of His body".

Considering all these facts, it is compelling to assume that Swami's reemergence could be the reason why most of the people would believe in Him. He then could be in this world for around 9 years. It is interesting to note that I also came across some Hadiths mentioning Mahdi will

---

[1]The Islamic calendar consists of 12 months in a year of 354 or 355 days. Since the age 95 could be considered as any time between age 95 and 96, the calculation based on 355 days gives an age between 93 and 94 of standard calendar years.

rule the world (after his rising) for 7 or 8 years (instead of 9).

> *Our Mahdi will have a broad forehead and a prominent nose. He will fill the earth with justice as it is filled with injustice and tyranny. He will rule for seven years.*
> - Bihar-ul-Anwar Vol.13 Part 1, English Translation p.143

> *[...]his reign will be seven years, otherwise eight, or otherwise nine.*
> - Bihar-ul-Anwar Vol.13 Part 1, English Translation p.143

> *(Mahdi) will fill the earth with equity and justice, as it shall be beset by injustice and oppression. The dwellers of the heavens and the earth will be happy from him. The heaven will not leave any of its blessings but descend it generously, the earth will not leave any of its plants but to bring it forth, so much so that the living ones will wish the dead. He will live in that for seven or eight or nine years.*
> - Bihar-ul-Anwar Vol.13 Part 1 English Translation p.91

These predictions bear an uncanny resemblance to the Nadi prediction about Swami's return:

> *At the age 88, people on earth will accept Him without doubt, blemish or shortcoming. He will live for 7 years.* (Gorakka Nadi, Reading conducted on June 14, 2011).
> - Sacred Nadi Readings, Sri Vasantha Sai, Page 26

> *He comes again and will remain only for 7 more years. Many changes will happen on earth during these seven years.* (Bogar Nadi, Reading conducted on May 25, 2011).
>
> - Sacred Nadi Readings, Sri Vasantha Sai, Page 18

Many Christians too believe that there will be a seven year period of joy and happiness that is often referred to as "The Rapture" (meaning state of being carried away with joy, love, or ecstasy). This period is believed to be ushered in by the second coming of Jesus Christ after which there will a 1000 year reign of peace in this world (More details in the chapter *"Dawning of the Sathya Sai Golden Age"*).

Mahdi's disappearance

Even from my early days as a Sai devotee, I have been reading various books on Swami where the Mahdi prophecies are mentioned. So I was always convinced that these predictions clearly pertained to the Sathya Sai Avatar. After I started writing this book a thought occurred to me that if those predictions were really about Swami, then there must certainly be some reference in those books to Swami's "early" disappearance as well. I decided to research myself what the various Hadiths had to say about this. I also obtained English translations of some of the volumes of Bihar-ul-Anwar and started reading them.

What I found in those volumes were mindboggling. I could not believe what I was reading. The Hadiths clearly talk about Mahdi's disappearance and eventual return! The Hadiths say that Mahdi will disappear twice from earth. First one will be for a long time and the second will be His actual disappearance (or death).

> *Hazrat Mahdi will disappear from sight for a time.*
> *- Bihar-ul-Anwar Vol.13 Part 1,*
> *English Translation p.133*

> *He will disappear twice. The first will be so long that some people will say that he is dead. Others will say that he has gone. Neither those who love him nor anyone else will know where he is[...]*
> *- Al-Muttaqi al-Hindi, Al-Burhan fi Alamat al-Mahdi*

> *By Allah, he (Mahdi) will disappear for years. He will be forgotten until it will be said: He is dead, perished or gone to some valley. The eyes of the believers will shed tears over him and they will be turned over like a ship is turned over by the waves of the sea[...]*
> *- Bihar-ul-Anwar Vol.13 Part 1,*
> *English Translation p.180*

The name Qaim (or Al-Qaim) has been used in many verses to refer to Mahdi which in Arabic means "Rising for Truth". Two things need to be noted here. First is the word "rising" which clearly points to an act of "ascension". Secondly, the word "Truth" which is the root meaning of Swami's partial name "Sathya" (as in Sathya Sai Baba). Further, Bihar-ul-Anwar calls this disappearance of Mahdi as the period of "occultation". The term occultation usually refers to celestial bodies (such as planets) to describe their temporary disappearance behind another planet. Here too the same term is used to describe Mahdi's temporary disappearance to an unknown realm. I saw many explanations given by different scholars about this period of occultation. Some even say that Mahdi will hide from humanity for hundreds of years and then appear before humanity just before the "end of times". But the verses in

CHAPTER 7: The Disappearance of Mahdi

Bihar-ul-Anwar paints a different picture altogether. One of the most interesting prophecies in Bihar-ul-Anwar is that when the Qaim rises, people will be wonderstruck thinking how this could happen because His body should have already decayed. This suggests that the act of occultation would begin with the disappearance of Qaim's body in an act of death.

[All the further verses in this chapter are taken from Bihar-ul-Anwar Vol.13 Part 1, English Translation unless otherwise specified]

> When the Qaim rises, people will say, How could this be? Even his bones must have decayed. (p.181)

> I said to him, "O son of Allah's Messenger, why is he called Qaim?" He said: "Because he will rise after the death of his remembrance[...]" (p.193)

> Behold, he will have an occultation during which the ignorant individuals will be perplexed and the invalidators will perish and the time-assigners will lie. Then he will rise. (p.193)

> I said: "Why is he called the Awaited?" He said: "He will have an occultation **the days of which will be many** and the duration of which will be long. The sincere will wait his uprise and the doubters will reject him and rejecters will mock at him. (p.193)

The above verse clearly states that the period of occultation would be a long one that would continue into many days. But the verses do not suggest that the period of disappearance would amount to hundreds of years as concluded by many scholars. Otherwise the verse would clearly have used the word "years" to identify such a long time. Also, please note the words "*rejecters will mock at* him". It is only a matter of fact that many non-believers have ridiculed it as a failed prediction that Swami left His body earlier than expected.

When will Mahdi return?

The return of Mahdi is expected to herald a new era of love and peace similar to the "Golden Age" mentioned in Swami's discourses. That day is mentioned in Islamic texts as *"yawm al-qiyamah"* which in Arabic literally means "the Day of Resurrection". It is also mentioned that no one knows when that day would come except God Himself.

> *O Messenger of Allah, when is the Qaim from your progeny going to rise?' He said: 'His example **is like the example of the Hour**: "...none but He shall manifest it at its time; **it will be momentous in the heavens and the earth**; it will not come on you **but of a sudden**.* (p.189)

The scripture says Mahdi's reappearance would be "sudden" in an unexpected moment that He alone knows the time of. This resembles the following verses in the New Testament that describes the coming of the "Son of man" (believed to be the second coming of Jesus Christ).

> *Watch therefore, for ye know neither the day nor the hour wherein the Son of man cometh.*
> - Matthew 25:6-13, KJV

> *But of that day and that hour knoweth no man, no, not the angels which are in heaven, neither the Son, but the Father.*
> - Mark 13:32, KJV

Mahdi to be back in a young body?

In the chapter "*Incredible Nadis*" we already saw Nadi prophecies that mention Swami's return. Some of the readings also mention that when He comes back He will assume a younger or middle aged body.

> *After He comes outside, He will have peace. He will continue with the task as He has done for the last 85 years.* ***Though the body will be younger, it will have the maturity and experience of 85 years.*** *He comes again and will remain only for 7 more years.* (Bogar Nadi, Reading conducted on May 25, 2011).
>
> - Sacred Nadi Readings, Sri Vasantha Sai, Page 18

Bihar-ul-Anwar also gives astonishingly similar clues:

> *What would be the sign of your Qaim when he reappears?* ***He replied: He will be advanced in age, but he will seem like a young man.*** *Whoever sees him will say that he is forty or less. The rotation of days and nights does not affect him till his last.* (Vol.13 Part 2 p.178)

Dr. John Hislop had published his record of an interview with Swami during which He mentioned: "*This body will live to age 96 and will remain young*"[1]. In Shakuntala Balu's book "*Living Divinity*", she mentions Swami's words: "*In this body, I will not become old or infirm as in my old (Shirdi) body*"[2].

---

[1] Conversations with Sathya Sai Baba, J.S.Hislop, Birth Day Publishing Co., San Diego, CA, 1978, Page 83 (mentioned interview is published only in this edition).

[2] Living Divinity, Shakuntala Balu, London Sawbridge, 1984, Page 40.

Are these statements indications that Swami will look younger when He is back?

We already discussed the verses in Bihar-ul-Anwar that says Mahdi will remain at least 7 years after His reappearance. I also found a prediction regarding Mahdi's final disappearance from earth:

> *He will remain seven years (after His reappearance) and then he will die and Muslims will pray over him (p.91)*

The Golden Age of Mahdi

Mahdi's arrival will be the precursor to a Golden era that will permeate the earth with peace and justice; the splendor of which is beautifully chronicled in Bihar-ul-Anwar:

> *By Allah...he will not go from the world until he appears and fills the earth with equity and justice, as it will be replete with injustice and oppression. (p.197)*

> *Blessed be you if you see his time! Blessed be anyone who sees his time! (p.170)*

> *And the earth will shine with the illumination of its Lord, and his rule will extend from east to west. (p.113)*

> *He will tear out the evil judges from you, cut away your dangers, and dismiss your unjust rulers, and will clean the earth from the dishonest. He will act with equity and establish amongst you a fair scale*

of justice. Your dead ones will wish they could return shortly once more and live again. This is to happen. For the sake of Allah, you are in your dreams! Safeguard your tongues and be after your livelihood, for depravity will come to you. And if you wait, you will be rewarded and you will find out with certainty that he is the avenger of your victimization and retriever of your rights. I take a true oath by Allah that Allah is verily with the people who are pious and who perform good deeds. (p.155-156)

At that time, the earth will reveal its treasures and show its blessings. Men will not find any place to give alms nor be generous, because wealth will encompass all the believers. (Part 2 p.233)

These verses explain the beauty of the prophesied Golden Age, the phenomenon of which seems to be exceedingly incomprehensible considering the current state of affairs in the world. But as we know, Swami who is the encompassment of all Divine principles and the Mahdi or Messiah who fulfills all eschatological prophecies has promised that the Golden Age will come. When it does, its beauty will be beyond all dreams and imagination:

The time is approaching when all humanity will live in harmony. That time will be here sooner than one expects. [...] It is not what anyone alive can imagine. It is beyond all comprehension. I can say that its beauty is magnificent beyond all dreams.

- Sri Sathya Sai Bal Vikas, Vol XV, No 9, Sept 96

Why will Mahdi return?

> *[...]because[...]he has not filled the earth with justice and equity, as predicted in the narrations, therefore, this must happen in the last period of time. These reasons have all combined to fulfill the declared destiny.* (p.141)

The above verse is of immense significance to the context of this book. It says since Mahdi has not yet fulfilled His predicted Mission to fill the earth with justice and equity, He is destined to return for its accomplishment. This is perfectly in consonance with the point that this book has been trying to make: Since many things that Swami has pronounced are yet to happen and many prophecies in the scriptures are yet to be fulfilled, He is sure to be back again!

> *[...]I am the security for the people on the face of the earth just as stars are security for the inhabitants of the heavens...Pray more for an early reappearance as in it lies your success.*(p.498)

CHAPTER 8:
A Vision in the Sky?

Many scriptures around the world foretell an event that will announce the arrival of the Lord on earth. One of the most popular and discussed-upon prophecies is the "Coming of the Son of man" in the New Testament of the Holy Bible. There are many verses in the Holy Bible that talk about Lord appearing in the sky at a most unexpected hour, thereby mesmerizing mankind into a spiritual submission.

> ***And then shall appear the sign of the Son of man in heaven:*** *and then shall all the tribes of the earth mourn,* ***and they shall see the Son of man coming in the clouds of heaven with power and great glory.*** *And he shall send his angels with a great sound of a trumpet, and they shall gather together his elect from the four winds, from one end of heaven to the other.*
> - Matthew 24:30-31, KJV

> ***For the Lord himself shall descend from heaven with a shout,*** *with the voice of the archangel, and with the trump of God[...]*
> - 1 Thessalonians 4:16-17, KJV

The above verses in the Holy Bible suggest a vision in the sky to be witnessed by mankind that would pronounce of God coming as the "Son of man". Many believe this to be the "Second coming" of Jesus Christ. However, according to Swami, Jesus had never mentioned about his own return. It was the coming of Baba that Jesus was always referring to.

> *[...]The statement of Christ is simple: "He who sent me among you will come again!" and he pointed to a Lamb. The Lamb is merely a symbol, a sign. It stands for the Voice Ba-Ba; the announcement was the Advent of Baba[...]Christ did not declare that he will come again. He said, "He who made me will come again". That Ba-ba is this Baba[...]*
>
> - Sathya Sai Speaks Volume 11 Chapter 54

Would it mean that the "second coming" of the "Son of man" in the Holy Bible refers to the second coming of Sri Sathya Sai Baba Himself? Could the world soon be witnessing a vision of the Sathya Sai form?

> **Behold, he cometh with clouds; and every eye shall see him**, and they also which pierced him: and all kindreds of the earth shall wail because of him. Even so, Amen.
>
> -Revelation 1:7, KJV

The Bible says every eye shall see Him during that vision which points to something of a global scale. There is an interesting prophecy from Agasthya Nadi on the reappearance of Swami mentioned in the book "*Sacred Nadi Readings*".

> *[...]Lord will give a vision of Himself in His present form. This will be a true vision of His real body.* **It will be seen by many who will be filled with wonder and amazement** *[...]Lord Shiva now tells that a vision will be seen* **not only in India but all over the world**. *It will be the same form,* **but in different places**. *Many people will be filled with wonder and claim to see him here and there. In fact,* **He will be seen in different places at the same time by many people**.
>
> - Sacred Nadi Readings, Sri Vasantha Sai, Page 18

CHAPTER 8: A Vision in the Sky?

Readings from the Agasthya Nadi certainly echo the gist of Biblical prophecies discussed above. The Bible also says that the "second coming" would be at an unexpected hour that no man would know of.

> *Therefore be ye also ready: for in **such an hour as ye think not** the Son of man cometh.*
> - Matthew 24:44, KJV
>
> ***But of that day and that hour knoweth no man**, no, not the angels which are in heaven, neither the Son, but the Father.*
> - Mark 13:32, KJV

We already discussed about the similarities in the coming of Mahdi or Qaim as mentioned in Bihar-ul-Anwar to the coming of the "Son of man" in Bible. Bihar-ul-Anwar also says that when Qaim rises after His disappearance, it will be at an unexpected moment. There are many verses mentioned in Bihar-ul-Anwar (about the reappearance) that resembles Biblical verses:

> *Behold, by Allah, your Mahdi will disappear from you [...] **Then he will come like a blazing meteor**. He will fill the earth with justice and equity as it will be full of injustice and oppression.*
> - Bihar-ul-Anwar Vol.13 Part 1, English Translation p.178

Now let us compare that to the Biblical verses that talk about the coming of the Son of man in the clouds akin to a lightning that strikes from east to west:

> ***For as the lightning cometh out of the east**, and shineth even unto the west; so shall also the coming of the Son of man be.*
> - Matthew 24:27, KJV

> *And then shall they see the **Son of man coming in the clouds** with great power and glory.*
>
> - Mark 13:26, KJV

These verses in the New Testament and Bihar-ul-Anwar further strengthen my belief that the world could witness a vision of the Sathya Sai form in the sky from multiple places. Readers would recall from the chapter *"Clues for His imminent return"* that some of the devotees have had dreams about Swami appearing in multiple places and many people around the world claiming to see Him. In the same chapter we had discussed about Seema Dewan's messages from Swami during His final moments in His body. I would like to examine the message *"I Have Gone Nowhere"* again in the light of above prophecies regarding the "vision in the sky" (excerpts only provided).

> *"[...]The devoted hearts with a pure mind and a loving heart shall call Me from time to time. They alone with the strength of their purity **shall make Me once again visible to the world and I will come once again with My hands full**. You must believe in My word for whatever I say never goes to waste. Whatever I say becomes truth. Always remember Me, know that I am before you. Free yourself from emotion and **await My return**".*

Swami says He will be once again "visible" to the world. Word "visible" is associated with vision. Was Swami giving a hint about a glorious vision that world is about to witness? Could that day of His reappearance with an astounding vision in the sky be the one that Swami suggested to be the "Day of Awakening"?

> ***The day of awakening** is not far away and **when it comes there will be a revelation of the true***

> power of God, a manifestation of omnipresence of the Lord.
> - Sri Sathya Sai Baba and the Future of Mankind, Satya Pal Ruhela, Page 223

Viswarupa Darshanam postponed

> *I never utter a word that does not have significance, or do a deed without beneficial consequence.*
> - The Life of Bhagavan Sri Sathya Sai Baba, N.Kasturi, Page 196

On Thursday October 4, 2007, it was announced (per Swami's direction) in Prasanthi Nilayam that Swami would be giving a *"Vishwarupa Darshanam"* (Vision of the Cosmic or Universal form) at around 7:00 PM on the northeastern direction of the Puttaparthi airport. As soon as this was announced, devotees started running towards the airport chanting His name. Television channels also telecasted the news and all the people in Puttaparthi locked up their houses and ran towards the airport. Thousands rushed to the area from surrounding villages as well. All the devotees crowding the area focused their attention on the northeastern direction in the sky. In a fit of devotion, some of them surrounded Swami's car and He could not even come outside. Devotees did not relent even after members of Sathya Sai Trust urged them to sit down. Instead they ran after the car.

A small stage was set up before the car for *Viswarupa Darshanam* but Swami could not even reach the stage as devotees prostrated before him. He was forced to remain in the car for about an hour. A short while later, the office-bearers of the Sathya Sai Trust announced that the *Viswarupa Darshanam* was postponed because of the non-cooperation of devotees and the cloudy weather. Swami then returned to His Ashram[1].

Now, that is a very intriguing episode indeed in the history of Sathya Sai Avatar because of its sheer uncharacteristic nature. It was very "un-Swami-like" that He would announce to give a public vision and then concoct a drama of postponing the same for whatever reason may it be. Swami was there to grant an astounding vision, that in itself a towering miracle to be. Then to postpone it because He could not get out of the car by inducing a minor miracle, transcends logic. But in the end we all know that Swami will not do anything without a valid reason.

Swami has granted celestial visions to many devotees in the past. However, those were only to certain individuals or a small group of people. One amazing such episode is narrated in the book *"Anyatha Sharanam Nasthi – Other Than You Refuge there is None"* by Sri Vijayakumari. The author recounts the amazing celestial visions that Swami granted to her and a few other devotees:

> *One day, when we were all walking towards the Chitravati, Swami suddenly disappeared. While we were searching for Him, we heard a clapping sound and, looking up, we found Swami alerting us, "I am on top of the hill." It was six in the evening. The sun had softened the streams of its rays and was sinking towards the west. The sky was filled with black clouds, as if it were wrapping itself in a thick blanket. Swami said, "You all look at me. I shall show you the sun."*

---

[1] Reference: www.ssso.net

CHAPTER 8: A Vision in the Sky?

Even as we were thinking, "how can the sun come back after it has already set?" we saw newly rising rays behind Swami's head. The whole sky was filled with blue clouds. The rays began to turn red till they looked fiery and exuded so much heat as to make us all sweat profusely. The rays were intensely hot as if coming from the scorching midday sun.

Unable to bear the heat we all made loud appeals, "Swami! It is too hot". The heat subsided. We were just settling down, when Swami's voice came down to us from the top of the hill, "I shall show you the Moon". We saw behind Swami's head, the half-unfolded honey-coloured rays of the moon. They soon turned white – whiter and whiter still. That was that. We began shivering in the cold. Our bodies became stiff. Our teeth began to chatter. "Swami! Cold! It's very cold, Swami!" As we were imploring Him thus, the cold slowly subsided.

While we were wondering what other miracle He would perform, He announced, "I shall show you the Third Eye. Watch it very carefully and attentively" "Third eye! How does it look?" we wondered. Swami's body was not visible. But His head appeared gigantic, as if it were stretched across the entire sky. Stupefied, great bewilderment filling our minds, we stared at the sky. On Swami's forehead, between His two eyebrows, an orifice appeared. Fiery, fuming sparks began to come out of the opening. Our eyes were dazzled by the brilliance of those sparks. We were scared. More than fear for ourselves, we were worried about what might be happening to Swami. The sparks continued to gush out. When we looked back, we found that many had fallen down, unconscious. We did not know what made them faint. That scared us further. We looked up, but could not find Swami anywhere. Feeling lost and not knowing what to do, we began weeping. Suddenly, we found Swami standing in our midst.

"What happened?" He asked us, patting us on our shoulders. "Why are you weeping? Why have these kids fainted?" Not knowing what answer to give to these questions, we just hugged Him and continued weeping.[...]

One by one, those who had fallen unconscious persons began to stir. It was a strange experience. We felt as if our bodies were moving unsteadily hither and thither. We felt as if we were floating on air. Some inexpressible joy seemed to pervade our entire being. [...]

We could not sing properly. We felt dizzy. That whole evening was spent in that state. When we found ourselves in a similar state the next day also, we asked Swami about it. He said with a smile, "You have been praying to have a glimpse of this Third Eye for many past lives. In answer to your prayers, today, I gave you darshan of it. But I did not show you even a thousandth part of its brilliance. You could not withstand even that. Your present state is the result of that spectacle." Overwhelmed by this revelation, we all broke down and wept. We washed His lotus feet with our tears [...]

- Anyatha Sharanam Nasthi, Sri Vijayakumari, Page 58-61

In the above episode, Swami tells the devotees that He did not even show a thousandth part of His brilliance. Even then the devotees could not stand the vision and fainted. Swami's effulgence is beyond all imagination. These reasons make the announcement and subsequent postponement of the above mentioned "*Viswarupa Darshanam*" even more intriguing. No one can really understand Swami's ways. But there are certain things we know of the Avatar; that He will not do anything without a valid reason. Whatever He does is for the benefit of mankind. Swami is not bound by anything at all. By the virtue of these "known" parameters, we can aspire to conceive the meaning of Swami's certain actions. If Swami says He will do something then He will definitely do it even though it is impossible for us to assume how and when it will happen. That is why Swami asks us to: *"Be Patient. In time, everything will be given to you"*[1]. For the same reason a Sai brother who was present during the *"Viswarupa Darshanam"* event, mentioned to me that he believes the whole drama was enacted as an indication of a Cosmic Vision that is to come in the future. It should also be noted that the Sathya Sai Trust (acting under Swami's directive) had announced the *"Viswarupa Darshanam"* to be "postponed" and not "cancelled".

Storm before the calm?

There is a peculiar prophecy from Agasthya Nadi mentioned in the "*Sacred Nadi Readings*" that foretells a great storm that would precede the vision of the Lord.

> *The Lords arrival will be preceded by a great thunderous storm. It may appear quite frightening, but it will stop quite suddenly and the vision of the Lord will take place. From this day onwards, great wonders will increase.*
>
> - Sacred Nadi Readings, Sri Vasantha Sai, Page 21-22

---

[1] Sanathana Sarathi October 1996 Back cover

In his book, Sai Messages for you and me, Lucas Ralli mentions Swami's message about a storm[1], after which there will be a completely new atmosphere that brings about peace in the entire world.

> *After the storm there will be a new beginning and the atmosphere will be completely different. It will be like a new age, the age of love, harmony and co-operation replacing the age of war, fighting, hatred, jealousy, greed and all those negative aspects of life.*
> - Sai Messages for You and Me Vol.I, Ralli, Lucas, 1985

When we analyze logically, Lords arrival could happen at a most opportune moment effectuating the protection of mankind from some calamity or catastrophe. In other words, Swami's reappearance or vision may not happen without such precursors. We already saw in the chapter "*Incredible Nadis*", Nostradamus quatrains that point to a natural phenomenon in the making.

So I believe, before the miraculous times can be experienced there might be a short period when the humanity could be forced to call upon the Lord in one voice for its protection. But from the above-mentioned Nadi prediction we can assume that even though the catastrophe would appear frightening, it would stop abruptly with the intervention of the Supreme Savior, our ever-loving compassionate Lord Sai.

A walk across the sky

Swami had mentioned to some of His close devotees that there will be a time when He would walk across the sky and people would then realize His Glory. He mentioned

---

[1] Could be metaphorical.

CHAPTER 8: A Vision in the Sky?

this in one of the public discourses as well.

I will have to move across the sky; yes, that too will happen, believe Me.
- Sathya Sai Speaks Volume 2 Chapter 18

You will realize Swami's glory when I walk across the sky from one end to the other.
-Thapovanam Sri Sathya Sai Sathcharithra, Ch.11

From the above events, it could be assumed that the "sky vision" was something that Swami always had in mind. How beautiful will it be when that happens! Blessed will be those who are fortunate enough to witness it.

PART 3

Thy Kingdom Come

CHAPTER 9:
Dawning of the Sathya Sai Golden Age

You do not know, so many great things are going to take place. Everything seen, heard or felt will turn sacred. All this is going to happen soon. Do not miss this sacred opportunity and waste it. Once lost you will never again get it. Once obtained you will never lose it.

- Divine Discourse, Prashanti Nilayam, October 14, 1999

Swami has often stated that He has come in order to inscribe a golden chapter in the history of humanity, thereby ushering in a "Golden Age", a new era of love, peace, righteousness and truth. Humanity is on the cusp of that peaceful and prosperous era in which there will be universal acceptance of the Sathya Sai Avatar with His name and form being established throughout the world.

Swami's quotes about this wonderful time to come are scattered over His numerous discourses. Some of the events may have already occurred partially. Also, a doubt may arise in our minds that some of these quotes could pertain to the times of Prema Sai Avatar. But we know from the general way of Swami's speaking that if He says "this form" or "this body", He clearly means His present Avatar as Sathya Sai Baba. Moreover, He has indicated directly and sometimes indirectly that the world would already be peaceful when Prema Sai arrives. Please see the following conversation that John Hislop had with

Swami during one of the interviews:

> JH: Many people are saying that, very shortly, we will enter a period of great catastrophe.
> SAI: There may be some peak waves, as I mentioned, but the world will be happy, peaceful, and prosperous.
> GUEST: No world war?
> SAI: No. No world war.
> JH: We are fortunate to be alive so that we may see this peaceful world.
> SAI: You will all see it. Even the old men will live to see it.
> **GUEST: Then Prema Sai will not have much work to do! Swami will have made the world peaceful.**
> **SAI: That is some 40 years away. At that time the world will be peaceful. That is the Name: Prema Sai. All will be love - love, love, love everywhere.**
>
> - My Baba and I, Dr. J.S.Hislop, Page 189
> From an interview in December 1978

In an interview to prominent journalist R.K.Karanjia, Swami explains that the mission of Prema Sai Avatar would be to make people realize that they themselves are God.

> "The mission of the present Avathar is to make everybody realize that the same God or divinity resides in everyone. People should respect, love and help each other irrespective of color or creed. Thus all work can become a way of worship. **Finally, Prema Sai, the third Avathar will promote the evangel news that not only does God reside in everybody, but everybody is God. That will be**

> *the final wisdom which will enable every man and woman to go to God"*
> -The Blitz Interview, September 1976

For Prema Sai Avatar to impart this knowledge to mankind, it being such advanced understanding that Swami calls "the final wisdom", wouldn't it be fair to assume that the humanity would have reached a reasonable level of spiritual awareness by that time? Who else could bring about that awareness other than the Sathya Sai Avatar Himself?

The Golden Age will recur

> *The Will of God cannot be stopped. The events God ordains must take place.* **The joyful Golden Age will recur.**
> *- An Eastern View of Jesus Christ, Page 12*

> *Many hesitate to believe that things will improve, that life will be happy for all and full of joy, and that the* **golden age will recur. Let me assure you that this dharmaswarupa, that this divine body, has not come in vain.** *It will succeed in averting the crisis that has come upon humanity.*
> *- Sai Baba, The Holy Man and the Psychiatrist, Page 91*

It will be here sooner than one expects

> *Fear not, My children, all will be well.* **Love and light will replace the darkness and a new era will be upon you very soon.**
> *- Sri Sathya Sai Baba and the Future of Mankind, Page 110*

The time is approaching when all humanity will live in harmony. That time will be here sooner than one expects. *Before it arrives, be prepared for whatever is needed to reveal to every living thing the true purpose of existence.* ***It is not what anyone alive can imagine. It is beyond all comprehension. I can say that its beauty is magnificent beyond all dreams.*** *And as each of you perform your silent work, I embrace you to My Heart and henceforth your souls shall be lifted up and your eyes will reveal My Presence within.*

- Sri Sathya Sai Bal Vikas, Vol XV, No 9, Sept.96

[...]The day when the brotherhood of man and the fatherhood of God will shine bright and beautiful is dawning and drawing near.

- Sathya Sai Speaks Volume 13 Chapter 18

[...]The whole world is today in the throes of anxiety and fear. But, I assure you that very soon the dark clouds shall be scattered and you will witness a happy era all over the world.

- Sathya Sai Speaks Volume 11 Chapter 28

When the world is on the verge of chaos, the Avathar comes to still the storm raging in the hearts of men. Prasanthi (the higher Peace, the calming of perturbations) will be stabilized soon; the demonic deviations from the straight Divine Path will be corrected. Dharma will be revived, and re-vitalized, in every human community.

- Sathya Sai Speaks Volume 11 Chapter 31

Nature of the Golden Age

> *When the Golden Age dawns there will be harmony throughout the world and love will flow everywhere. All thoughts of hatred will disappear. Today you cannot visualize such a state because there is chaos everywhere, fighting, scheming, hatred, evil; all the negative emotions are in the ascendent. But eventually the change will come.*
> - Sai Messages for You and Me Vol.II, Page 70

> *If there is a change, **it will be a universal change**. Not local. **It will occur every place**.*
> - My Baba and I, Page 189

> *[...]The day[...]when the whole humanity gets unified as one big family observing strictly the principles of Truth, Righteousness, Love, Peace and Non-violence[...] will mark the **establishment of the Sai Rashtra and blessed indeed are those who will be able to experience that Heaven on earth**.*
> - Sai Vandana, 25, 1990

> *It will be like a new age, the age of love, harmony and cooperation replacing the age of war, fighting, hatred, jealousy, greed and all those negative aspects of life.*
> - Sri Sathya Sai Baba and the Future of Mankind, Page 223

> *Love and peace will [...] cleanse the horrors and excesses of the dark ages which today pollute the very atmosphere.*
> - Sri Sathya Sai Baba and the Future of Mankind, Page 10

Life will change, it will improve and you will experience a richness in the quality of life which has eluded you in the past.

- Sri Sathya Sai Baba and the Future of Mankind, Page 221

Today we find acts of violence everywhere. But whatever is happening, in a way, is for your own good. **Everyone will develop sacred feelings. All will enjoy the divine bliss. The entire nation will enjoy peace and happiness soon. There will not be any difficulties or suffering.**

- Divine Discourse, Brindavan, March 16, 2003

Avatars do not succeed or fail; what they will must occur; what they plan must take place... **I have come to inscribe a golden chapter in the history of humanity, wherein falsehood will fail, truth will triumph, and virtue will reign. Character will confer power then, not knowledge, or inventive skill, or wealth. Wisdom will be enthroned in the councils of nations.**

- Sathya Sai Baba, Embodiment of Love, Page 174

Universal acceptance of Sathya Sai Avatar

My name and form will soon be found getting established everywhere. They will occupy every inch of the world.

- God Descends on Earth, Page 37

You are going to witness the divine glory of Swami unfolding in the days to come. He will attract the whole world. There won't be place for people to stand even.

- Divine Discourse, Brindavan, March 16, 2003

CHAPTER 9: Dawning of the Sathya Sai Golden Age

Do not consider Sai Baba as a mere figure five feet three inches tall. **His Presence will be felt all over the world. Wait and see. In a few days the entire world will come here.**
- Sathya Sai Speaks Volume 28 Chapter 19

Let alone America, Puttaparthi is going to be a name to be reckoned with in every major developed country in the world such as Japan, Germany, Italy, France etc. Everywhere world maps are going to mark Puttaparthi as an important location.
- Divine Discourse, Prasanthi Nilayam, October 19, 1999

Swami answers to the question what sign will He give that the Golden Age is beginning that **the glory of Sai will spread to every part of the world. It will increase a thousand fold.**
- Sanathana Sarathi, December 1993

In a matter of a few days you will come to know. **The divine glory will increase day by day, conferring on you joy and bliss. All the unrest will soon be eradicated from the face of earth.**
- Divine Discourse, Brindavan, March 16, 2003

*[...]***The day when millions will gather to benefit from the Avatar is fast coming**; *I am advising you to garner and treasure all the Grace and all the Bliss you can, while you may[...]*
- Sathya Sai Speaks Volume 11 Chapter 41

Importance of the Sai Organization

> The Sai Organization may be limited in size now, but as time goes on, **it will attract so many people that the general public will not be able to be accommodated in the Sai gatherings. All available spaces will be assigned to the people within the Sai Organization.** Thus, the Sai Organization membership affords a chance.
>
> - My Baba and I by Dr. J.S.Hislop, Page 209
> From an interview in December 1982

Even beyond that:

> **The whole world will be transformed into Sathya Sai Organisation and Sathya Sai will be installed in the hearts of one and all."**
>
> - Sanathana Sarathi, January 1999, Page 16

The Glory of Bharath (India)

> **Again how fortunate you are that you can witness all the countries of the world paying homage to India (Bharatha); you can hear adoration of Sathya Sai's name reverberating throughout the world, even while this body is existing** --not at some future date but when it is with you, before you. **And again, you can witness very soon the restoration of the Ancient and Eternal Religion (Sanathana Dharma) to its genuine and natural status, the righteousness (dharma) laid down in the Vedas for the good of all the peoples of the world.** The revival of vedic dharma is the Sai Sankalpa (the resolve that Sai has) not only drawing people toward me, attracting

them by the manifestation of my shakti (power) and samarthya (capacity).
- Divine Discourse, May 17, 1968

India will be the leader of the world in all respects - spiritually, culturally, socially, politically and economically. *All her past glory, culture and traditions will be revived and she will shine forth as the leading nation of the world. This is how it was yugas (ages) ago and this is how it will be once more.*
- Sathya Sai Amrita Varshini, Page 34

Today is Krishna Janmashtami, the birthday of Lord Krishna. ***I am making a promise today that the people of all the countries, viz. Pakistan, China, Germany, Russia will be united[...]The goodness of Bharat will lead to this unity.***
- Sanathana Sarathi, September 2002

We can only imagine and try to conceptualize the beauty of the much anticipated Golden Age which according to Swami will be "magnificent beyond all dreams". Swami cites the bad state of affairs around us as the reason why we are not able to comprehend that such a beautiful time would recur. But He promises it will come.

[Prof.Kasturi:] Let us wait joyfully for the new world order, the Perfect Sai Order, not in a far off future, but very soon, sooner than any human mind can comprehend, looking at the present state of affairs in all walks of life.
- Sanathana Sarathi, August 1991

Significance of the year 2012

The whole world is abuzz with talks of the year 2012 and the nearing of apocalyptic end times. Many sections of the media have also tried to cash in on the various speculations and doomsday predictions, flaring up the flames of fear among the masses. The frenzy around the 2012 mystery focuses on the ancient Mayan calendar that mysteriously ends with the winter solstice on December 21, 2012. Some astronomers have also predicted a "galactic alignment" which is believed to occur along the end of 2012 when our solar system passes directly through the Galactic Equator. In the opinion of some, these signs portend the end of times.

Even though I do not believe in the "end of times" theory, I feel that the hype itself has some significance. Many people around the world are expecting something to happen in or around the year 2012 even though nobody really knows what is in store or to expect. No one seems to agree on whether it will be good or bad either. But we know that nothing extremely cataclysmic could be around the corner since Swami Himself has assured us:

> *No disaster is imminent for the world. Over the vast globe, there may be some mishaps here and there, from time to time.*
>
> - Sathya Sai Speaks Volume 24 Chapter 4

On the other hand there are also many who believe that the year 2012 could be the beginning of a spiritual regeneration of planet earth rather than the end of times itself. They perceive the signs as precursors to a massive transformation of global consciousness. Whatever may be the case, there must be some justification to such collective expectation around the world, the foundations of which cannot be discounted as insignificant. It is interesting to note that Dr. Srikanth Sola, an internationally reputed cardiologist currently serving at the Sri Sathya Sai Institute of Higher Medical Sciences, Whitefield, Bangalore, mentioned in a RadioSai interview:

> *I remember once back in 2007 Swami was in Kodaikanal, this was shared with me by some of His students. And Swami just casually remarked "**Sathya yuga begins in 2012**". He said it as casually as if He would say it rains during monsoon season and so we know that we're at the end of one age and at the beginning of the next[1].*

The above statement certainly provides an indication about the significance of the year 2012. Most importantly, any miracle of Swami to occur around these "uncertain" times is sure to receive world-wide attention with much of humanity already engrossed in the anticipation of something substantial. Perceiving from that angle, I am tempted to believe that this so-called "2012 paranoia" could also be a product of divine contrivance. So the year 2012 could signify an end after all; the end of all evil and injustice as we know today, marking the commencement of a beautiful Golden Age as prophesied by many scriptures.

The Golden Age according to Scriptures

In Brahma-vaivarta Purana Part 4 Krishna-janma-khanda, Chapter 129 is called Golokarohanam, because it describes how Krishna returns to His abode (at the end of Dwapara Yuga), the Goloka or Vaikunda. In that there is a specific dialogue between Lord Krishna and Mother

---
[1] Interview published in media.radiosai.org on May 28, 2012

Ganga (Ganges). Verse 49 is a question by Ganga, Verses 50-60 are Krishna's answers. Below are the translations of some of these verses:

> Verse 49: *Ganges said: O protector, Supreme enjoyer, on your departure for the perfect abode, Goloka, thereafter what will be my situation in the age of Kali?*
>
> Verse 50: *The Supreme Personality of Godhead (Lord Krishna) said: On the earth 5,000 years of Kali will be sinful and sinners will deposit their sins in you by bathing.*

Lord Krishna tells Mother Ganga that for the first 5000 years of Kali Yuga, there will be many sinners and there will be a lot of sufferings. Mother Ganga proceeds to ask the Lord as to what would happen after those 5000 years. The Lord replies:

> Verse 55: *O Ganges, the whole planet will become a pilgrimage place by the presence of Vaisnavas, even though it had been sinful.*
>
> Verse 56: *In the body of My devotees remains eternally [the purifier]. Mother Earth becomes pure by the dust of the feet of My devotees.*
>
> Verse 57: *It will be the same in the case of pilgrimage sites and the whole world. Those intelligent worshipers of My mantra who partake My remnants will purify everything.*

After around 5000 years of Kali Yuga, Lord Krishna says there will be a period when the whole planet will be transformed to a pilgrimage place due to the presence of His devotees or *Vaisnavas* (literal meaning "worshippers

CHAPTER 9: Dawning of the Sathya Sai Golden Age

of Lord Vishnu" but contextual meaning is "devotees" or "spiritual aspirants") all over the world. Lord Krishna proceeds to mention that this period would last thousands of years.

According to Swami *"Eleven thousand years is the full length of the Kali yuga.[...]Kali yuga still has 5,320 years before ending."*[1]. More than 5000 years have passed in the Kali Yuga which would mean that we are into the glorious period that Lord Krishna was referring to. In his book "Sai Baba Avatar", Howard Murphet writes about a passage in the great epic Mahabharata where Sage Markandeya meets the Pandavas in the forest during their exile. Sage Markandeya talks about the conversation he had with Lord Vishnu about a time during the darkest period of the Kali Age when human values would deteriorate, violence and injustice would be widespread, falsehood would triumph over truth, oppression and crime would be prevalent. Lord Vishnu tells Sage Markandeya that He would take a human birth in the Kali Yuga in order to intervene and set the world on a new course to establish the "Sathya Yuga" or the Age of Truth:

> *"When evil is rampant upon this earth, I will take birth in the family of a virtuous man, and assume a human body to restore tranquility by the extermination of all evils; for the preservation of rectitude and morality, I will assume an inconceivable human form when the season for action comes. In the Kali Age of sin I will assume an Avatar form that is dark in color. I will be born in a family in South India. This Avatar will possess great energy, great intelligence and great powers. Material objects needed for this Avatar's mission*

---

[1] Conversations with Bhagavan Sri Sathya Sai Baba Page 27-28

> will be at his disposal as soon as He will think of them. He will be victorious with the strength of virtue. He will restore order and peace in the world. This Avatar will inaugurate a new Era of Truth, and will be surrounded by spiritual people. He will roam over the earth adored by the spiritual people."
>
> "The people of the earth will imitate this Avatar's conduct, and there will be prosperity and peace. Men will once more betake themselves to the practice of religious rites. Educational centers for the cultivation of Brahmic lore, and temples, will reappear again everywhere. Ashrams will be filled with men of Truth. Rulers of the earth will govern their kingdoms virtuously. The Avatar will have an illustrious reputation."

-Sai Baba Avatar, Page 71

These words of Lord Vishnu as Sage Markandeya recollects, clearly describes the characteristics of Sathya Sai Avatar. It also talks about how the Avatar would restore order and peace in the world, spiritual education centers and places of worship would spring everywhere and there will be virtuous rulers in all countries.

In Brahma-vaivarta Purana, as we saw earlier, Lord Krishna mentions that the world will be filled with His devotees whose very presence would transform this earth into a place of pilgrimage. This points to a massive expansion of the "critical mass" constituting the spiritual consciousness of this world to be brought about by more and more people turning towards God. It is only prudent to assume that the ensuing Golden Age will be brought about by Lord Sai Krishna Himself, transforming the whole world with His love, might and Divine Grace into one big Sai Organization.

> The whole world will be transformed into Sathya Sai Organisation and Sathya Sai will be installed in the hearts of one and all.
>
> - Sanathana Sarathi, January 1999, Page 16

Coming of the Son of Man

Examine the following words of Jesus to His disciples:

> I have yet many things to say unto you, but ye cannot bear them now. Howbeit **when he, the Spirit of truth, is come, he will guide you into all truth [...]**
>
> - John 16:12-13, KJV

"Spirit of Truth"? Who else other than Sri Sathya Sai Baba that Jesus could have been referring to? On the Christmas Eve of 1972, Swami made a startling revelation, overwhelming the Christian world by declaring that He was the one who had sent Jesus Christ to this earth:

> There is one point that I cannot but bring to your special notice today. At the moment when Jesus was merging in the Supreme Principle of Divinity, He communicated some news to his followers, which has been interpreted in a variety of ways by commentators and those who relish the piling of writings on writings and meanings upon meanings, until it all swells up into a huge mess.
>
> The statement itself has been manipulated and tangled into a conundrum. **The statement of Christ is simple: "He who sent me among you will come again!"** and he pointed to a Lamb. The Lamb is merely a symbol, a sign. It stands for the

Voice Ba-Ba; the announcement was the Advent of Baba. **"His Name will be Truth"**, *Christ declared.* **Sathya means Truth.** *"***He will wear a robe of red, a blood red robe.***" (Here Baba pointed to the robe He was wearing!). "***He will be short, with a crown (of hair). The Lamb is the sign and symbol of Love***".*

Christ did not declare that he will come again. He said, "He who made me will come again." **That Baba is this Baba and Sai, the short, curly-hair-crowned red-robed Baba, is come.** *He is not only in this Form, but, he is in every one of you, as the dweller in the Heart. He is there, short, with a robe of the colour of the blood that fills it.*

- Sathya Sai Speaks Volume 11 Chapter 54

Swami's words mentioned above perfectly accord with the vision of St.John as explained in the Book of Revelations (In New Testament of the Holy Bible):

And I saw heaven opened, and behold a white horse; and he that sat upon him was called **Faithful and True**, *and in righteousness he doth judge and make war.* **His eyes were as a flame of fire, and on his head were many crowns**; *and he had a name written, that no man knew, but he himself.* **And he was clothed with a vesture dipped in blood: and his name is called The Word of God**. *And the armies which were in heaven followed him upon white horses,* **clothed in fine linen, white and clean. And out of his mouth goeth a sharp sword, that with it he should smite the nations: and he shall rule them with a rod of iron:** *and he treadeth the winepress of the fierceness and wrath of Almighty God. And he hath on his vesture and on*

his thigh a name written, **KING OF KINGS, AND LORD OF LORDS.**
- Revelation 19:11-16, KJV

St.John calls the rider of the symbolic white horse (white symbolizes peace and horse symbolizes power and far-reaching command) as "Faithful and True". This matches with Swami's partial name "Sathya" which means Truth. Blazing eyes are one of Swami's prominent features and His hair does look like a crown. The robe dipped in blood points to the red or orange robe that Swami wears. "*His name is called the Word of God*" incidentally points to the meaning of the word "Bhagawan". The power of Swami's discourses is symbolized as the sharp sword coming out of His mouth. His will-power and authority is mentioned as "rod of iron". Does it not match the Hindu prophecies regarding the coming of Lord Kalki riding a white horse wielding the sword? Of course, the horse and the sword are symbolisms as mentioned earlier. It is to be noted that St.John refers to Him as the *"King of Kings and Lord of Lords".* This also matches the description in Nadi prophecy *"When the Kali Yuga influence grows even more intense, then people will see His true might and will acknowledge that He is the Supreme Power. Then mankind will bow to him as to a great emperor."*

St. John also sees a multitude of people numbering into millions who have gathered around the throne of the Son of man.

And I beheld, and I heard the voice of many angels round about the throne and the beasts and the elders: **and the number of them was ten thousand times ten thousand, and thousands of thousands.**
- Revelation 5:11, KJV

Now let us compare that to Swami's own words:

> *[...]**The day when millions will gather to benefit from the Avatar is fast coming**; I am advising you to garner and treasure all the Grace and all the Bliss you can, while you may[...]*
> - Sathya Sai Speaks Volume 11 Chapter 41

There are many verses in the New Testament regarding the coming of "Son of man" that Christians believe to be the second coming of Jesus Christ. But we already saw Swami's words where He says that Jesus had not mentioned about his own return. It was the coming of "Baba" that Jesus was referring to. Could it mean that the "second coming" of the "Son of man" in the Holy Bible refers to the second coming of Sri Sathya Sai Baba Himself?

> *When the Son of man shall come in his glory, and all the holy angels with him, then shall he sit upon the throne of his glory. And before him shall be gathered all nations: [...]*
> Matthew 25:31-34, KJV

The coming of "Son of man" is believed to herald a new era of truth, love and peace similar to the Golden Age mentioned in Swami's discourses.

> *The Son of man shall send forth his angels, and they shall gather out of his kingdom all things that offend, and them which do iniquity.*
> - Matthew 13:40-43, KJV

The Son of man and His angels will abolish all evil to ensure righteousness and peace in the new Kingdom. This golden period where evil, falsehood, hatred and disharmony will be completely absent, is said to last at least 1000 years:

> And I saw an angel come down from heaven, having the key of the bottomless pit and a great chain in his hand. And he laid hold on the dragon, that old serpent, **which is the Devil, and Satan, and bound him a thousand years**, And cast him into the bottomless pit, and shut him up, and set a seal upon him, that he should deceive the nations no more, till the thousand years should be fulfilled:
> - Revelation 20:1-3

In St.John's vision, he sees the angel binding the devil away for a thousand years. This is symbolic of all evil, untruth and disharmony being cast away from earth. What follows is another resplendent vision in which St.John sees a beautiful new city descending from heaven that becomes the center of this peaceful world.

> And I John saw **the holy city, New Jerusalem, coming down from God out of heaven,** prepared as a bride adorned for her husband. And I heard a great voice out of heaven saying, **Behold, the tabernacle of God is with men, and he will dwell with them, and they shall be his people, and God himself shall be with them, and be their God. And God shall wipe away all tears from their eyes; and there shall be no more death, neither sorrow, nor crying, neither shall there be any more pain: for the former things are passed away.**
> - Revelation 21:2-4

St.John sees this new city from heaven where God who has descended as the "Son of man" would dwell in along with His people. He would wipe all sorrow from the face of this earth and there will be no more fear of death. St.John calls this city "The New Jerusalem". The name "Jerusalem" in Hebrew literally translates as "dwelling of peace" (Ref:Wikipedia). Isn't that the same meaning as "Prasanthi Nilayam" too? Was St.John's vision a glimpse to the future of Prasanthi Nilayam, the abode of supreme peace? The city which Swami says the whole world will be obliged to come to?

> In the days ahead, **the whole world will be obliged to come to Prasanthi Nilayam.**
> - Sanathana Sarathi, December 1991

> **You will witness Puttaparthi becoming a Madhura Nagara** (birth place of Krishna). No one can stop this development or delay it.
> - Divine Discourse, Prasanthi Nilayam, October 21, 1961

> Believe me, this Puttaparthi is soon to become a Tirupathi [...] **The reestablishment of Sanathana Dharma will emanate from here.**
> - Sathyam Shivam Sundaram Part 1 Chapter 16

Interestingly, according to Hindu prophecies, Lord Kalki is expected to come in a city called "Shambala" which literally translates as "place of peace, tranquility and happiness" (Ref:Wikipedia).

Let us all wait for that defining moment in the history of mankind when the heavenly city of Prasanthi Nilayam where the Lord Himself is to reside would become the epicenter of a major spiritual upheaval, proclaiming the dawning of the Sathya Sai Golden Age.

*Be patient. In time everything will be given to you. Be happy. There is no need to worry about anything.[...]***You are all sacred souls and you will have your parts to play in the unfolding drama of newer Golden Age, which is coming.**

- Sanathana Sarathi, October 1996, Back cover

CHAPTER 10:
Why did Swami leave His body?

No one can understand my Mystery. The best you can do is to get immersed in it.
- Sathya Sai Baba, The Embodiment of Love, Page 96

Nobody knows why Swami had to leave His body earlier than expected. It must have been part of His plan all along. All we know is only what we have seen and heard so far. His body was becoming weaker and weaker and with all vital organs failing one by one, it came to a point where it had to be abandoned. Now the question may arise as to why He did not cure Himself. Such questions are beyond us and are part of the great mystery that Swami is. Only answer is that He willed it so and it was meant to be that way. Nothing has ever been left to chance; He is *"the master of all"*.

This body has come for the sake of devotees

*[...]an illness assumed, willed, in order to relieve a person who could not have survived it or even borne it without perturbation. This is one of the functions of the Divine, for which it has incarnated - the pouring of Grace on the devotee[...]***I have come with this body in order to save these other bodies from pain and suffering***. This body will ever be free from illness and pain; disease can never affect it. That is the real truth.*
- Sathya Sai Speaks Volume 10 Chapter 37

From the above words of Swami, it is quite evident that whatever illness He had to suffer did not originate in His own body. The Law of Karma works in very mysterious ways. One thing is certain that once the action (or thought) goes forth, the result or the "fruit" is imminent. It is also true that the *"karmic debt"* can be willfully received by one person from another. Swami has taken up the *karma* of His devotees many times since they could not have handled the effects themselves. Even though He could have negated any *karma* by His will alone, Swami chose not to. Instead He took the devotees' *karma* upon Himself. Having taken a human body, Swami has always respected the *karmic* laws even though He Himself was unaffected by it.

> *Any instant solution would go against the fundamental quality of nature itself as well against the karmic law of cause and effect.*
>
> - The Blitz Interview, September 1976

Previously whenever He had taken up the *karma* of a devotee, His body had gone through some sufferings albeit only for a short period of time. But this time did our ever-loving compassionate Lord decide to take up the *karma* of the entire humanity and burn it with each and every cell in His body? He lived His whole life with the sole mission of uplifting the mankind and sacrificed His body for the same cause as well?

Once in an interview to prominent journalist R.K. Karanjia, Swami pointed out that the natural calamities were the direct results of collective *karma* or evil deeds of man.

> *Suffering and misery are the inescapable acts of the Cosmic drama. God does not decree these*

> calamities, but man invites them by way of retribution for his own evil deeds.
> - The Blitz Interview, September 1976

Swami had touched upon this subject on other occasions as well:

> [...]Man is deriving innumerable debt from Nature, and enjoying the amenities provided by Nature in various ways. But what is the gratitude he is showing to Nature? What gratitude is he offering to the Divine? He is forgetting the Divine who is the provider of everything. That is the reason for his becoming a prey to various difficulties and calamities[...]
> - Sathya Sai Speaks Volume 21 Chapter 19

> [...]Many natural catastrophes are entirely due to man's behaviour. Earthquake, volcanic eruptions, wars, floods and famines and other calamities are the result of grave disorders in Nature. These disorders are traceable to man's conduct. Man has not recognised the integral relationship between humanity and the world of Nature[...]
> - Sathya Sai Speaks Volume 25 Chapter 37

In *karmic* theories this is referred to as "mass *karma*". Bhagawan has stated that averting such large-scale natural and manmade calamities including nuclear holocausts are part of His mission. If calamities are the direct results of collective *karma*, wouldn't averting those calamities require clearing of such *karma* as well? Was Swami absorbing a huge critical mass of *karma* in order to prevent some major disasters? When we examine carefully the various world events that were unfolding during the time Swami was hospitalized, it is not difficult

CHAPTER 10: Why did Swami leave His body?

to find a connection. He was taken to hospital with breathing difficulty (or pneumonia) a few days after the Japan earthquake/tsunami/nuclear disaster. The triple disaster was an extremely unfortunate event that claimed thousands of lives (peace be with them) and rendered many homeless and sick. The largest earthquake in Japan's history along with a fierce tsunami it triggered, destroyed parts of Fukushima nuclear power plant and the country was bracing itself for a possible nuclear catastrophe. The Fukushima reactors were designed for worst-case anticipated earthquake magnitude of 8.2 Richter scale but the actual earthquake exceeded that (9.0 Richter scale). Some experts say that it was a miracle that the plant withstood the event and that it was possible to avoid a complete "melt-down" of the reactor. In short if the complete melt-down had occurred, the disaster could have assumed unimaginable proportions; something of the scale that is yet to be witnessed by humanity. That was about something we know of but how are we to know about the disasters that were destined to happen yet never did? He alone knows! At this juncture I am reminded of the *Shuka Nadi* prophecy: *"He will show that he alone can control the fury of nature"*.

Swami has made it very clear that whatever happens to His body is only for the welfare of humanity.

> *As Narsimhamurthi pointed out Kasturi once urged Me not to neglect this body in the process of saving a devotee.* **I replied that this body has come for the sake of devotees and shall be utilized for doing anything and everything for their welfare.** *Body attachment is human and total detachment is divine. Attachment to the body is responsible for all suffering and misery. Since God does not have any body attachment, He does not*

attach any importance to the suffering of His body. ***Once He assumes a body, many things are bound to happen to the body. Whatever happens is for the welfare of the whole world.***
- Divine Discourse, Prasanthi Nilayam, January 14, 1999

What more proof do we need? All we need to understand is that His body was sacrificed "***for the welfare of the whole world***". As mentioned in the above quote from His discourse, He did not attach any importance to the suffering of His body. Swami could go to any extent in order to save a devotee as He would later reveal in the very same discourse:

> [In my own humble opinion, this should be regarded as one of Swami's landmark discourses that every Sai devotee should read]
>
> *While returning from Bangalore (in the month of December),* **I instructed the Warden NOT to bring the boys for sports meet.** *They attributed various reasons to this word of Mine[...]Students are tender hearted, full of noble feelings and love for Swami. They planned various programs with a view to please Me.* **I was very well aware of the impending danger. But, students were not receptive to My words.** *I felt there was no point in advising them in such a situation. Only when they face the consequences of disobeying My command do they realize the value of My words. Till this moment nobody is aware of what exactly happened on the 11th morning. They said that the sports meet was a grand success. I am also happy when you are successful. Students performed extremely well. Each contributed to the success of this event based on his*

CHAPTER 10: Why did Swami leave His body?

capacities and capabilities. That morning as I entered the stadium, I spotted two lorries. Immediately I could visualize the danger lurking in the corner. I saw the lorries with huge scaffolding placed over them. The boys planned to perform a few acrobatic feats on them. I knew that one of the rods was not fitted properly and was about to give in. **If that were to happen the boy would suffer a major head injury and spinal breakdown. I willed that the boy should be saved and decided to take it upon Myself**[...]A day prior to that I had instructed four boys to surround the chariot and keep a vigil. They are also full of love and devotion for Swami. But I noticed that none of them were present at that spot. Nobody is to be blamed. No one does this deliberately. Swami is the very life-breath of the students.

I asked for the chariot to be stopped. A senior devotee was driving the chariot with all sincerity, love and devotion. He stopped the vehicle in accordance with My command. Just when I was about to speak to the Vice Chancellor, the driver accidentally put his foot on the clutch instead of applying the brake. **That resulted in a jerk and I fell down on the chariot. As a result I suffered injuries on my head, hand and My spinal column was badly damaged. What the boys had to face, I took it upon Myself.** Many men and women were seated in the gallery, but I took care that none noticed My injuries. I pretended as though nothing had happened. The Vice Chancellor was worried thinking that Swami was unable to get up. **I knew that any further delay would cause anxiety in the minds of devotees. So, I immediately got up forgetting the pain and started blessing the**

devotees waving My hands. The pain was so intense and the cut on My hand so deep as though it was pierced with a knife. But the sleeve of the robe covering My hand was intact. This incident gives you a glimpse of the infinite power of Divinity.

I found Myself in an awkward situation. I had to walk up to the dais without My injuries being noticed. ***So I willed that no one should notice My injuries, lest they become anxious.*** *I walked up to the dais and took My seat. But in the meanwhile the dhoti below the robe was drenched in blood. Concerned that the devotees may get to know of this I walked into the bathroom discreetly. The available towels were insufficient to wipe the oozing blood. I did not want to leave the bloodstained towels in the bathroom, lest someone notices them. Though there was excruciating pain, I washed the towels Myself with soap, squeezed them and put them up for drying. Under no circumstances do I reveal My suffering, pain and fatigue. Some boys were curious to know why I went to the bathroom repeatedly. I replied, "Why are you concerned? It is My job?" Usually I go to the bathroom only twice a day, morning and evening. Since it was bleeding profusely, I had to go to the bathroom 5-6 times in that short duration. In the meantime two students came and prayed that the flag may be hoisted. When I got down from the chair the sensation was such that it seemed as though I was subjected to electric shock. Reflecting on the incident I feel like laughing to Myself. I could not stand firmly on the ground. I thought I should not be deluded by the attachment to the body and walked forward smilingly to hoist the flag. Then I lighted the lamp. I*

CHAPTER 10: Why did Swami leave His body?   131

found Myself in an embarrassing situation. I could not sit in any posture comfortably. When I exhort all devotees to give up body attachment, I should set an example Myself in this regard. Saying to Myself in this manner I conducted myself accordingly.

The Primary School children performed extremely well and desired to have a photograph with Me. Acceding to their prayers I walked up to them and took photograph, as I did not want to disappoint them. Subsequently I had to walk up to the play field five more times to take photographs with remaining students. In this manner I detached Myself from the body. My body was numb. There was no sensation whatsoever. My head was reeling. **I resolved to make them happy no matter what happened to the body. I decided to keep this to Myself.** Concerned that the bloodstains may be visible while returning to the dais from the playground, I ascended the steps leading directly to My seat. **Is it possible for a human being to conceal such a major injury from the public gaze for a long time being amidst such a huge gathering? No.** I was seated on the chair for five long hours. **I am relating all this so that students and devotees may comprehend the nature of divinity. Anyone in My predicament would not have been in a position to sit in the chair even for a second. It would have been impossible even to put a step forward. It was as though the electric shock was piercing My body.** It is the electric current, which gives shock, but when I am the current Myself, where is the question of Myself being subjected to shock?

With that feeling I sat through the whole proceedings and returned to the Mandir. The

Central Trust members followed Me, but they were not aware of what had happened to Me. The senior devotee apologized for what had happened. Then I told him, "why do you worry about the past? Past is past. I am happy. Do not worry about Me." All of them had their lunch. After the lunch it started bleeding again. All the students were waiting outside for photographs. Again I went into the bathroom to wipe the blood. Noting this Indulal Shah cried out, "Swami, what is this?" I told him lovingly, "Indulal Shah, whatever had to happen to the body has happened", saying so I showed him My injury. All of them cried out in agony. They noticed blood all over. I told them that I would not reveal anything in future if they expressed their sorrow like this. No one knew about it until I reached the Mandir. **Likewise, I take upon Myself the untold suffering of students and devotees at various points of time in order to protect them.** *No one is responsible for this mishap. You may find fault with one individual or other, but no one is responsible for this. Whatever had to happen, happened. That's all.*

I am narrating this episode only to affirm the fact that I go to any extent to protect My devotees who obey My commands. *When I returned to the Mandir I called those four boys. They noticed My injuries and were crestfallen. I chided them for not obeying My command. I asked them, "Why were you not present there at that time as commanded by Me? If only you had obeyed My command, this incident would not have occurred." I told them not to feel sorry about it.*

- Divine Discourse, Prasanthi Nilayam,
January 14, 1999

CHAPTER 10: Why did Swami leave His body?

As Swami finished His discourse, emotions ran amock; devotees sobbed, students wept. Not only did Swami take up the grievous injury, He also painstakingly hid it from devotees in order to make sure that the proceedings were not disrupted. He sat through the whole program even with that excruciating pain just to satisfy His devotees. How can words describe Swami's Love for us? Even though the students were not receptive to His words, He still protected them. Swami with His infinite Love of thousand mothers, never made any compromise when it came to the wellbeing of His devotees. How blessed are we to be in His Love!

To understand the magnanimity of Swami's "final act" with His body, let us muse over a popular story of how Swami cured a student who had asthma by transferring the disease to Himself. One of the students of Vrindavan was suffering from a severe case of Asthma. He had been writing letters and praying to Swami for relief from his ailment. During one of the evening Darshans, Swami went straight to the boy and held his hand. In a moment the students found Swami was breathing hard. Realizing that Swami was taking over his disease, the boy cried out: *"Baba, I wanted you to cure me, not take my disease on you. Please don't suffer for my sake."* Saying so, he tried to free himself from Swami's grip. But Swami held on for two minutes and then started breathing normally. Then He looked at the boy deeply and said:

> Do you think I need your letters to know what's happening with you? I knew about your asthma. Your karmic effect got transferred to me. **20 years of suffering for you is only 2 minutes of suffering for me.**

If twenty years of a person's suffering was only two minutes of suffering for Him, how can we even attempt to comprehend the amount of *karma* that the Loving Lord took upon Himself for those twenty-eight days that He was in the hospital? And this is not counting the many days, weeks and months before that when He was said to be silently enduring!

The power of prayers

> *Remember that there is nothing in this world as powerful as the Lord's name to protect it. It is not arms and bombs that will save the world. Only God's grace should protect the world. It is man's foremost duty to pray for God's grace. Prayer is of supreme importance.*
> - Sathya Sai Speaks Volume 24 Chapter 4

> *Through genuine prayer, mountains of evil can be pulverised and destroyed.*
> - Sathya Sai Speaks Volume 13 Chapter 26

While Swami was in the hospital all devotees were fervently praying for Him to cure Himself. There were continuous prayer sessions and mantra chanting being held in all parts of the world. Each and every Sai devotee had only one thing in mind, that is Swami's health. If I just take my case, never had I prayed with so one-pointed attention and yearning as much as I did in those twenty-eight days. That should have been the case for each and every Sai devotee I presume. Just by the virtue of that concerted effort from Sai devotees during those few days, the positive vibrations in the world could have gone up by a significant proportion. In one of the messages to Seema Dewan (please see the chapter *"Clues for His imminent return"*) named *"For your sake only"* that she received on April 4, 2011, Swami gives a revelatory message (excerpts only provided).

> "[...]**The name of the Divine when chanted frees the negative energy that continuously hovers over the world today.** I am always in bliss even when my body undergoes turmoil. I do not feel pain... I only remember you... your safety... and I remain in bliss. You remember Me most in times of trouble. But how can I give you trouble? I am your Mother. I always look for your welfare. To see one tear of yours makes me rush to be by your side. I am always by your side. You are not able to see Me for your eyes look for this world.
>
> You are nothing but Me. **To drive away the negative energy you must remember the name of God. That is why I have taken upon Myself this sickness. You remember Me... pray and remain in a clean pure frame of mind by that. Just by that positive energy emanates from you and all the troubles and catastrophes that you or your loved ones are about to face are washed out.**
>
> As for Me the ailment of the body is nothing. **You endure pain when you see Me like this and from it you derive strength in order to pray, love, unite, and do the right thing. That is all that I want for your sake.** Your peace lies in goodness alone.
>
> [...]Even the siblings who fight come together when the Mother's body is ailing. **I want to see you united with love for each other with complete unity and have faith that you are under the umbrella of My protection**"

Swami clearly cites His wish that the devotees pray hard in order to rid the world of negative energy. Were all the chanting and prayers actually redirected to ensure the welfare of this Universe? Taking up the sickness was probably Swami's way to get His devotees united in their prayers. When Mother Sai fell ill, all His children came together united to pray for Him. Even after Swami has left, the bond within the Sai family has multiplied tenfold. Everyone has felt the need to look out for each other. The devotion has increased. Sai activities have increased. Everyone feels Swami is closer to them than ever before. People could go beyond the body consciousness and identify Him as the *"Hridayavasi"*, the indweller of their hearts.

News that travelled far and wide

Mark Twain once said: *"A lie can travel halfway around the world, while truth puts on its shoes"*. Same is the case with unpleasant news too. Very quickly it spreads far and wide. Many people around the world actually came to know of Swami through the news of His leaving the body. It is interesting to note that for a few days Swami's passing was one of the top international story on Google news and seventh biggest story of 2011 according to Time magazine. Some people who had negative information on Swami could have even changed their outlook seeing the way the Indian Government honored Him with a state send off.

On the other hand, there has been a lot of negative publicity too. Devotees living outside India may have encountered people enquiring about the Guru who had recently passed away in India (most of the people in India do know Him). More importantly, they might have been curious to know how His prediction to live till 96 had

CHAPTER 10: Why did Swami leave His body?

failed. There has been scathing attacks by various groups against the Sai fraternity even from the time when Swami was hospitalized. While Sai devotees were fervently praying to Him to cure Himself, those people kept questioning how someone who could fall ill and get hospitalized can be considered God. After Swami left His body, while the devotees were expectantly waiting for Him to return, even some sections of the global media came down scoffing at our faith. Nevertheless, most importantly His name has been spreading far and wide across the world for whatever reasons may it be. Now imagine when Swami comes back, most of the people would have already heard about Him and the supposedly failed prediction!

In my opinion, all the negative propaganda has really been serving a purpose and probably bears the imprint of a divine design. When various people with their own selfish motives try to tarnish His name and as they unyieldingly decry the faith of His devotees, in my own craving mind I can envision a divine drama unfolding, a thunderous riposte that is taking shape in the subtle expanses of this cosmos.

> [...] Even those who are not now able to recognize the truth of Swami will have to approach with tears of repentance and experience Me. Very soon, this will be worldwide.
> - Sathya Sai Speaks Volume 15 Chapter 55

How can a play be enjoyable without some low points? A writer scripting a play makes sure to include some setbacks for the main character so that in the end the audience may exult in the character's renaissance or victory. In this Divine Play scripted and directed by Swami Himself, why wouldn't He include His own twists and turns? So that His devotees who have surrendered everything at His Divine Lotus Feet may exult in the ecstasy of His final victory?

> *This (Divine) phenomenon will sustain truth, it will uproot untruth, and in **that victory make all of you exult in ecstasy.** This is the Sai Sankalpa (Will).*
>
> - Divine Discourse, May 17, 1968

Many things in one stroke

> ***I shall certainly achieve the purpose of this Avathar, do not doubt it. I will take My own time to carry out My plan. So far as you are concerned, I cannot hurry because you are hurrying. I may, some time, wait until I can achieve ten things in one stroke**; just as an engine is not used to haul one coach, but waits until sufficient haulage in proportion to its capacity is ready. **My word will never fail; It must happen as I Will.***
>
> - Sathya Sai Speaks Volume 1 Chapter 31

We have discussed many reasons deduced from Swami's own words on why Swami could have left His body. There was a golden age yet to come. Calamities had to be averted. For that the collective *karma* and the negative energy had to be driven out. How was that possible? Through taking up the *karma* in His body and making the devotees to pray. It does not stop there. How to intensify the devotion and *sadhana* of His devotees? How to make them more united? How to make them realize that Sai is not just a body; He is in everything and everybody? Not only that, many people have come to know of Him through the news of His leaving the body. He left fittingly on an Easter day (Please see the chapter *"The Glory of Resurrection"*). Swami mentioned He sometimes waits until He can achieve ten things in one stroke. But between His hospitalization and eventual leaving the body, He probably achieved a twenty!

There is no need to worry about anything. Whatever is experienced, whatever happens, know that this Avatar willed it so. There is no force on earth, which can delay for an instance the Mission for which this avatar has come.

- Sanathana Sarathi, October 1996, Back cover

CHAPTER 11:
The Glory of Resurrection

Followers of Jesus believe that He suffered and died on the cross in order to absorb the sins of His disciples. Swami also has mentioned that Jesus sacrificed His life for the sake of His followers.

> *To take upon Myself the sufferings of those who have surrendered to Me is My duty. I have no suffering and you have no reason to suffer too when I do this duty of Mine. The entire give-and-take is the Play of Love. It is taken over by Me in Love; so how can I suffer?* ***Christ sacrificed His life for the sake of those who put their faith in Him. He propagated the truth that service is God, sacrifice is God.***
> - Baba, Sathya Sai Part 2, Page 171

We know from the Holy Bible that Jesus had resurrected Himself on the third day after crucifixion. The same body that perished while serving the purpose of absorbing the *karma* was reinstated back to life with His divine powers. But we know only a little about Jesus' activities after resurrection. There are instances mentioned in the Holy Bible where He gave visions of the resurrected body to His close disciples. What else did He do after that? Let us refer to an excerpt from the book "*Sathya Sai Baba, The Embodiment of Love*" by Peggy Mason & Ron Laing.

> *I was anxious to ask Baba one question. So, I said:*
>
> *"Swami, there's something I've wanted to know for a long time. Did the physical body of Jesus recover in*

CHAPTER 11: The Glory of Resurrection

> the tomb? I mean, it wasn't a materialised body of spirit - in the same way that Yogananda's Master (Swami Sri Yukteswar Giri) showed himself to him in fully materialised form three months after he had been buried?"
>
> Swami replied, "No - the physical body. No spirit materialised body. The physical."
>
> "Ah!" I said. "Then, did he journey to the East, continuing his mission to Kashmir?"
>
> "Yes - and he also travelled to Calcutta, and Malaysia."
>
> "Then is it the body of Jesus which was buried in the Rozabal Shrine at Srinagar in Kashmir?"
>
> Swami nodded, and said "Yes"[...]
>
> - Sathya Sai Baba, The Embodiment of Love,
> Page 48-49

The book talks about an interview that Peggy Mason had with Swami during which she asks Him whether Jesus had resurrected the actual physical body or it was a materialized one. Swami replies that it was the actual physical body. Then Swami goes on to confirm what many researchers had only speculated till then. That after resurrection, Jesus had travelled to India and that the tomb of Rozabal Shrine in Srinagar (Jammu & Kashmir, India) is indeed His. Body of Jesus (who was known in that part of the world as Yuz Asaf – "Yuz" meaning son of Joseph) is believed to have been buried there after the actual physical death. Jesus is also believed to have spent many years after resurrection as a spiritual master.

Peggy Mason's interview with Swami also has a reference to the case of Swami Sri Yukteswar Giri who resurrected three months after His death and showed Himself before His disciple Sri Paramahansa Yogananda. As Swami Himself confirms indirectly, Sri Yukteswar Giri's resurrection was in a materialized body, so two types of resurrection are being discussed. Shirdi Sai Baba also had left His body only to re-enter it in three days time. What is important is that the act of resurrection has been the part and parcel of the mission of holy beings who incarnate on earth from time to time. But when we look from a different perspective, it is the actually the act of death that glorifies resurrection. If there is no death, then there is no resurrection. In fact, that one single act of Jesus is responsible for earning Him the faith of billions of people who follow Him today. In 1 Corinthians 15 (New Testament), St.Paul explains in detail the importance of the resurrection of Christ.

> *If Christ be not risen, then is our preaching vain, and your faith is also vain.*
> - 1 Corinthians 15:14, KJV

St.Paul's commentary can be summarized as "to believe in resurrection is to believe in God". Because If God really does exist and if He had created the universe, then He also has power to raise the dead. Only He who gives life can resurrect it after death. St.Paul goes on to explain that if there was no resurrection, then there would be no use preaching about Christ. The act of resurrection is the pillar on which the roof of Christianity rests upon. It is also considered the greatest miracle Jesus had ever performed. In the Islamic faith, the day when Mahdi the promised teacher is expected to rise is regarded as *"yawm al-qiyamah"* which in Arabic literally means "the Day of Resurrection". When Swami talks about the "new

CHAPTER 11: The Glory of Resurrection

coming" that will herald a new Golden Age (please see the chapter *"Clues for His imminent return"*), was He referring to a miracle of similar kind? Why did Swami choose the Easter day[1] that is considered to be the day of Jesus' resurrection in order to leave His body? Was He giving us another hint that the same thing will happen in Sai Avatar too? Sri B.K.Mishra a Sai devotee who has authored and translated several books on Swami firmly expresses his belief[2]:

> *He (Swami) is a divine soul. He has just discarded his mortal body. In fact, his death on Easter day indicates that he may resurrect just like Christ.*

Question of a body

> *You are surprised that I can be in two bodies at the same time, or in a thousand different places.*
> - Sathyam Sivam Sundaram Part 4, Page 194

During those few days after Swami left, many thoughts had passed through my mind. Would Swami resurrect Himself in a few days like Jesus did? If He were to resurrect that soon, why did He then have to leave the body at all? Swami had indicated that His divinity would be revealed to the world through an event. Maybe the resurrection would serve that purpose? But then would the world really accept it? (On a lighter note: Now when I think of it, had Swami returned in two or three days time, probably the law-enforcement would have gone after the Sathya Sai Trust thinking they enacted a drama of death

---

[1] Commemorating the significance of Swami choosing the Easter Day for His leaving and in anticipation of His imminent return, the first edition of this book is published on April 8th, the Easter day of 2012.

[2] As per his statement to a Newspaper Ahmedabad Mirror dated April 25, 2011.

and resurrection in order to dazzle the devotees and rest of the world. This is unfortunately not the times of Jesus Christ or Shirdi Sai Baba!). If Swami is to resurrect, does He really need that same body in order to do so? Does that have to happen before the body decays? There were many such questions that I had asked myself. But the truth is that there cannot be any reasoning at all when it comes to Swami and His inscrutable ways. Swami the Lord of Lords is beyond time and space. For Him to recreate a body would be as easy as picking up a blade of grass.

> *There is nothing that Divine Power cannot accomplish. It can transmute earth into sky and sky into earth. To doubt this is to prove that you are too weak to grasp the grandeur of the Universal.*
>
> - Sathya Sai Speaks Volume 4 Chapter 49

Even while Swami was in His body, there have been instances where He had appeared in multiple places at the same time. One such instance that comes to mind is the experience of Sri K.N.P.Nayar, a businessman to whose house in London Swami visited in His subtle body On June 6, 1993[1]. Not only did Swami stay in his house for around four days, He even went on a sightseeing trip with Sri Nayar and his wife. The body was a real one that Sri Nayar and wife could touch and feel. All the while His physical body was still in Prasanthi Nilayam engaged in business as usual. This is only one of many such instances when Swami has been in two (or more) bodies at the same time. Now the question is which body was the real one? The one that was doing routines in Prasanthi Nilayam or the one spending time with a devotee in

---

[1] Reference: Video interview of Sri K.N.P.Nayar by Ted Henry & Jody Cleary – souljourns.net.

another part of the world? Or both? Which body is the one that was laid to rest in His *Mahasamadhi*? We do not have an answer. The point is that even while Swami was in His body, He was not restricted to one physical body alone. Why would there be any restrictions now even after He has left one of them?

Swami mentions in *Ramakatha Rasavahini*, how it was the pseudo-Sita or maya-Sita that was abducted by Ravana and not the real Sita. The actual Sita would never have been able to be touched by Ravana but the drama had to go on in order to fulfill the purpose of Rama Avatar. The maya body of Sita played along till the act was over and the original Sita was then recovered back by Lord Rama from fire after Ravana's death. For all purposes, the maya body followed the same human traits and demeanors as required by the divine drama and there was no real difference in the absolute physical sense. When Swami explains such subtle truths from previous Avatars, He indeed gives pointers to the behavior of Avatars in general including Himself. In the chapter "*Incredible Nadis*" we saw some Nadis referring to Swami's maya body and we have also seen Mahdi prophesies that point to Mahdi's disappearance that appears to be death. So it could be possible that Swami's leaving the body was only an illusion to the outside world and in that case His return could be the revelation or reappearance of His actual body!

The concept of Nirmana Kayas

One of the ultimate yogic powers defined as "Niramana Kaya" (literal meaning materialization of the body) is the ability to recreate bodies even after the death of the physical one. Select yogis are believed to possess this ability. I found this explanation from Sadhguru Jaggi Vasudev of Isha Foundation[1]:

> *There have been many yogis in the past, who still are in some ways, they retain their subtlest part of their body intact and then let it be. Whenever they feel it is necessary, they are capable of recreating their old bodies[...] Such people are known as "Nirmana Kayas" who recreate their own body. Gautama, the Budha is supposed to be one of the Nirmana Kayas. There are many others who recreate their own body as it was then, a youthful body as they liked it[...]Time is not an issue.*

If yogis have the power to recreate their bodies, can not the bestower of all powers do it too? I guess the question has never been whether Swami can do it or not. It has been whether Swami would choose to do it. Many argue that since Swami respects the laws of nature, He may not be inclined to go against them. Doesn't that suggest Jesus was doing something against the law of nature too? Nevertheless, I can narrate so many incidents where Swami has already transcended the natural laws. Swami Himself has confirmed this to be the case. Let us consider the following quote from Swami:

> *Some elders try to confuse you.* **Krishna showed many wonders, with an amazing disregard of the laws of nature** *and so, according to them, He had to meet death from the arrow of a hunter! Jesus, they say suffered crucifixion, for, He too manifested many miracles! Their argument is that,* **since I am defying the laws of nature***, I too will suffer likewise! They hope to create panic and spread*

---

[1] Reference: www.ishafoundation.org – From video of a talk given by Sadhguru Jaggi Vasudev.

alarm. But, these are the prattlings of weakness, ignorance and envy. ***They cannot understand this Glory, nor do they desire to tolerate it!***

- Sathyam Shivam Sundaram Part 3 Chapter 8

In the above words, Swami indirectly confirms that Lord Krishna, Jesus and Himself, have all transcended the laws of nature. Avatars are not affected by anything. Every Avatar had to go beyond natural laws in order to accomplish their mission. In fact, there have been defining moments in the career of all Avatars where extraordinary feats were performed so that people could hail those as the manifestations of divinity, compose songs about, sing them and meditate upon the Glory. Lord Krishna lifted the Gowardhana Mountain to protect the village from excessive rain when He was still a child. He also reconstructed and gave life to the body of His Guru's son who was dead for twelve long years. Lord Krishna had performed many such astounding feats including the destruction of the planet Naraka that once came close to hitting the earth[1]. In the Sai Avatar too, He has performed countless mindboggling miracles including resurrection of devotees, stopping rain and flood, curing diseases and even teleporting devotees across continents. In fact, all His miracles would seem to be beyond the laws of nature. Isn't that why they are called "miracles" in the first place?

During an interview with Swami, prominent journalist R.K.Karanjia asks Him the reason why God should assume human form? Swami answers:

---

[1] *"At one time, the Naraka planet appeared to be approaching close to the earth. The inhabitants of the earth were filled with dread of the approaching catastrophe. They prayed to the Lord for averting the imminent disaster and saving them. At that stage, Sri Krishna used his extraordinary knowledge (Prajnaa) to destroy the planet".*

- Sathya Sai Speaks Volume 24 Chapter 26

> Because that is the only way to incarnate the God within man. The Avathar takes the human form and behaves in a human way so that humanity can feel kinship with divinity. **At the same time He rises to godly heights so that mankind also can aspire to reach God.** The realization of the indwelling God as the motivator of life is the task for which Avathars come in human form.
>
> -The Blitz Interview, September 1976

Even the Godly acts were examples in order to remind people of their own divinity. That they can do the same things if they too would rise to the same level. That is why Jesus says:

> Verily, verily, I say unto you, He that believeth on me, the works that I do shall he do also; and greater works than these shall he do; because I go unto my Father.
>
> - John 14:12, KJV

What does Swami Himself say about resurrection?

> What is the resurrection, really? It is the revelation of the divinity inherent in man.
>
> - Divine Discourse February 28, 1964

Swami lived His life as an example to this world. His miracles have been reminders to all of us about our own inherent potentials. That is why Swami always says "*I am God and you are God too*". So the belief against His reappearance by transcending the laws of nature is completely unfounded. In fact, it would only be a befitting adornment to the Glory of the greatest Avatar ever to have walked this earth!

CHAPTER 12:
Conclusion

Many indications have been provided in this book on the possibility of Swami's imminent return. However, I also believe that it is the faith and prayer of His devotees that will bring Him back. Swami once said that He is even ready to part with Prasanthi Nilayam to meet the needs of His devotees.

> *I am prepared even to part with Prasanthi Nilayam to meet your requests. I am prepared to do anything for the good of the people. That is My only concern.*
>
> \- Sai Vaani, Messages collected from discourses of Sri Sathya Sai Baba

We know what Swami meant but no one expected that He would literally part physically with Prasanthi Nilayam. I am certain that it was done for the sake of the whole world (for reasons discussed in Chapter *"Why did Swami leave His body"*). So if He is to return, that will also be for the same sake alone. For that the first step the devotees need to take, in my humble opinion, is to believe wholeheartedly in Swami's words with unwavering faith and pray for His return. During one of Swami's initial declarations of His Avatarhood, He had stated *"Sadhus (Spiritual aspirants) prayed and I have come"*. The advent of Sathya Sai Avatar has been prophesied in various scriptures from thousands of years ago. But still the *Sadhus* had to pray for Him to descend. So is it not logical to assume that we devotees need to pray fervently for Him to be back? Swami once said to one of His devotees:

> *Yes, I keep my word to those who are steady in their faith.*
>
> - Sathyam Sivam Sundaram Part 4 Page 181

We now know that having complete faith is the key. The main reason for publishing this book is to build a consensus among the devotees to have faith and unanimously pray for Swami's return. I have no ulterior motives or hidden agenda. The online (internet) edition of this book is made available for free reading as well. One thing I would like to insist through this book is that **to believe in Swami's return is not a weakness. In fact, having unflinching faith in Guru's words is considered the strength of a disciple or a devotee.** However, one should not question his or her Guru's ways. Whatever Swami does, He alone knows the meaning of or reason for. We are not to question that. But it is our right to have complete faith in His words because that is what Swami urges us to do:

> *Truth is the life of the plighted word. My words bear the imprint of truth. I cannot depart from truth. I don't speak to those who attach no value to My words.[...]When people heed My words, I am ready to help them in every way and confer happiness on them.*
>
> - Sathya Sai Speaks Volume 28 Chapter 2

Swami instructs all to attach full value to His words. How then can we devotees be selective as to which words of His to believe in and which not to? We devotees try to limit Him into our own perception of what He can and cannot do. Instead of believing in the certainty of Swami's words, we try to fit whatever has already happened into a vague and obscure interpretation of them. We tend to

CHAPTER 12: Conclusion

forget that this is the very same God that created the whole universe and whatever else there is. Can He be limited to anything? Most of the devotees believed during the initial days after Swami left that He would resurrect Himself. Because going by Swami's own words, it was not time for Him to leave yet. Why then now believe otherwise? What has changed since then? If He could come back then, what would stop Him from coming back now? He was not limited to that body anyway! It is our duty to have complete faith in all His words. I am certain it is such unwavering faith alone that will bring Him back.

I found my own faith about Swami's return echoed in an interview given to RadioSai (posted on February 15, 2012) by Sri Vinod Cartic, an alumnus of Sri Sathya Sai Institute of Higher learning who was a gold medalist in MBA from the same institute. He shares his convictions in the interview[1] (excerpts only provided):

> *[...]On a personal note, I share a conviction which - again, I cannot explain - it is just intuition that of course Swami is Omnipresent;* **He is always here, but I am absolutely, 200% sure that we will see Him physically again. I have no doubt about this.**
>
> *Swami has said a lot of things; I don't think we need to actually lessen our faith for different reasons. Swami keeps every single word of His.* **The whole Universe has to re-orient itself to fulfill His Word. Let's all remember, that we are talking about God incarnate and not someone ordinary.**
>
> *From my experience, if there is one essential*

---
[1] From media.radiosai.org/journals/vol_10/01FEB12/04_vinod_04.htm

learning as far as the physical aspect of Swami is concerned, **I know that the voice of Swami is also the voice of the conscience.** There has never been a dilemma where Swami has said something and the conscience is saying something else. **This is why I say with complete conviction that every single thing that He has said will prove itself in time.**

Swami will keep all promises

Swami has said that He will fulfill all His promises whatever the circumstances may be. During the early years of Sathya Sai Avatar there is a story of Sri Subbamma, a devotee whose house served as the gathering place for devotees to have Swami's *Darshan*. She had immense love and devotion towards the Lord. Swami had promised her that He would satisfy her one desire, that is to have the *Darshan* of Baba in her last moments. When Subbamma died, Swami was not in Puttaparthi. However the relatives had kept the body till Swami returned on the next day. How Swami fulfilled her last wish is a thrilling story that He Himself narrates:

> *[...]people came running to Me and said, "Swami, Your Subbamma passed away last night." Immediately, I turned the car and went to Bukkapatnam straightaway. Her body was kept in the verandah, covered with a cloth. The entire household was griefstricken.* ***Once Swami makes a promise, He will certainly fulfill it under any circumstances.*** *I removed the cloth covering the body. As she had passed away the previous night, ants were crawling all over her body. I called out, "Subbamma," and she opened her eyes. This news spread like wildfire within no time. The people of*

CHAPTER 12: Conclusion

> *Bukkapatnam started crowding the place telling each other that Subbamma was brought back to life. Subbamma's mother was a hundred years old at that time. I told her to bring a glass of water with a Tulasi leaf (holy basil) soaked in it. I put the Tulasi leaf in Subbamma's mouth and made her drink some water. I said, "Subbamma, I have kept up My promise. Now, you may close your eyes peacefully." She said, "Swami, what more do I need? I am leaving blissfully." Shedding tears of joy, she held My hands and breathed her last.* **This is how I keep My promise under any circumstances. In this manner, I never go back on My promise.*
>
> - Divine Discourse, October 20, 2002

Swami called Subbamma's soul back temporarily in order to grant her the last *Darshan*. This event is a testimony to the fact that Swami fulfills all promises no matter what happens. If Swami could bring His devotee back to life just to fulfill the promise of a final *Darshan*, what stops Him from bringing Himself back in order to fulfill His own words?

I have not even the slightest doubt that Swami's words, ones that are not already, will eventually be fulfilled. How and when, Swami alone knows! Only in a few years time when we look back we will come to understand. Sri Sathya Sai Baba is not an ordinary Avatar. We are talking about the most powerful manifestation of God as human ever on this earth! Many years from now, when the future generation would read about the Glory of Sathya Sai Avatar, there will not be any trace of even a single failed prophecy amidst all the glorious encomiums. I refuse to believe that there will be!

A training period for His devotees?

When Swami left, all the devotees were grief stricken. As though to prepare us for that event, Swami had given a unique assurance:

> *Nobody needs to be worried or anxious about Swami's wellbeing. No danger can ever befall Swami. Swami will always come out of all difficulties and troubles unscathed; none need to fear or feel sorry or sad. Swami will achieve all success.*
> — Divine Discourse, July 13, 2003

The above statement is very relevant because Swami, whilst acknowledging that difficulties and troubles will be ahead, also assures us that He will come out of them unscathed. But how can we not be anxious or worried? It is our beloved Swami! Swami says when Krishna left His body, Arjuna was not able to bear that separation and lost his mental strength.

> *Arjuna always felt that Krishna was in his heart and that gave him his strength. When he heard that Krishna had died, he felt that Krishna was gone and as he felt this his strength left him.*
> — Conversations with Sathya Sai Baba, Page 159

Even in *Dwapara Yuga* when an advanced devotee like Arjuna could not bear the separation from his Lord, how are we in this *Kali Yuga* to cope up with such agony? However, with Swami's Grace, it is also true that many of the devotees have moved on and tried to go beyond the form and install Swami in their hearts. In my belief that is also a part of His Divine play to help His devotees overcome the attachment to His form and body.

CHAPTER 12: Conclusion

Accordingly, even as we yearn fervently for His return, we need to make sure that our prayers are not intended towards regaining His physical proximity. Such a prayer would only defeat the whole purpose of why Swami has made Himself disappear in the first place. In previous chapters we already saw Swami's statements about His longevity and how the Sathya Sai Avatar would usher in a Golden Age in this world. Had Swami not made those statements, we would probably all be expecting the Prema Sai Avatar right now and not the return of Sathya Sai Avatar. For the same reason, we should all pray from the perspective of the elevating impact that Swami's return will have on the whole world given the dire situation that it is in right now.

As Swami has mentioned many times, all His devotees have parts to play in His Divine Mission.

> *All of you should play a part in bringing forward the transformation (leading to the Golden Age) and the instrument you should use is Love.*
> - Sri Sathya Sai Baba and the Future of Mankind, Page 224

Even as early as in 1979, Swami through a message to Charles Penn, instructs all of us to be ready and prepared to become instruments in His Mission.

> *Your mission has begun. Those are My words to you, My devotees. Each of you has a unique and valuable part to play in this lifetime. Only those whom I have called can serve Me. My Mission has now reached that point in time when each of you now has work to do. This planet has a purpose in the great galaxy in which it is held. That purpose is now unfolding before our eyes. I call upon you to radiate the*

Bhakti (devotion) within you so that its unseen power will envelop all who come into your orbit. To successfully perform your part, always remain centred upon Me[...]The multiplication of My Love will be felt throughout the world. I have prepared you for this work over many incarnations. I have drawn you to Me. I have made great steps in My Mission over these past incarnations. My work is ceaseless and so your work, too, is without end. [...]

Know that I am within and without you. There is no difference. Rid yourselves of the petty matters forevermore. You are now in Me and I am now in Thee. There is no difference. My Darshan (spiritual blessings) will pour forth from Me to and through you. You may be unaware of this constant action. Be ever pure of heart and soul and mankind in your lifetime will benefit from your unique qualities.

Others, too, will join Me in this Mission when I draw them to Me. The time is approaching when all humanity will live in harmony. That time will be here sooner than one expects. Before it arrives be prepared for whatever is needed to reveal to every living thing the true purpose of existence[...]

- My Beloved, Charles Penn, Page 96-97

Rather than waiting for Swami's return in order to continue His work, each devotee should intensify his or her *sadhana* and crave for becoming His divine instruments in the new Sai Age that is to unfold before us. That is what Swami urges us in the above thought-provoking message.

Even during the early times when Swami was readily accessible to devotees, I have heard stories where He had

CHAPTER 12: Conclusion

distanced His physical self from some close devotees to whom once He had given so much personal attention. As I understand, what prompts Swami to do it is His motherly love and eagerness to make the devotees rid themselves of their attachment to His form and realize the oneness with His formless reality, which is sometimes difficult when you are in His physical presence. I believe it is for the same reason that He has forced His temporary disappearance upon us; so we learn the most important lesson that Swami is not just a physical body and that He is always above us, around us and in us. With that realization, we should turn inward and prepare ourselves for the beautiful spiritual era that lies ahead as Swami has promised.

On the other hand, when Swami comes back, can we even imagine the measure of impact that it will have on this world? Swami once said that the whole world would come to Prasanthi Nilayam and there would not be any place to stand even[1]. Dr.K.Hanumanthappa describes his dream about the future of Puttaparthi in his book *Sri Sathya Sai Baba A Yugavatar* (Page 167)[2].

> *Only on festival occasions one can have darshan of Swamy from a far off place. Even then we cannot see the full physical figure of Swamy. So in future, this will be the unpredictable situation. We old devotees feel as though we are in a strange world.*

So it is only appropriate that we devotees try to see Him in our hearts rather than crave for His physical proximity which could be near to impossible anyways. In the chapter *"Disappearance of Mahdi"* we already saw how

---

[1] Please refer to Chapter *"Dawning of the Sathya Sai Golden Age"*
[2] Please refer to Chapter *"Clues for His imminent Return"*

the prophecies about Mahdi completely match the characteristics of Sathya Sai Avatar. We also saw what has been written about Mahdi's disappearance and eventual reappearance. I also came across another interesting prediction which says that Mahdi will not have any allegiance to anyone when He returns.

> *When he rises, our Qaim will not have allegiance to anyone on his shoulders.*
>
> — Bihar-ul-Anwar Vol.13 Part 1, English Translation p.147

In other words, when the Qaim or Mahdi rises after the disappearance, it will not be for the sake of any particular section of people. Rather He will be the Lord of this whole world. Probably this time of His disappearance is a training period for us devotees to cope with such non-attachment?

Swami has always been inhibiting His powers behind the veil of His *maya* and humanness. His reasoning was that if He did allow His actual powers to manifest, the whole world would come to Him but the time was not ripe for that yet.

> *That time (for public declaration of Avatarhood) is still far off. Prior to that I have to bring such persons near me, who, in their previous lives, have been incessantly and untiringly trying to get access to me through their severe sadhana. A time will come when the world will know about the Avatar through public declaration[...]*
>
> — Sai Baba and Nara Narayan Gufa Ashram, Part II, Page 38

CHAPTER 12: Conclusion

> *As days pass, even those who are not now able to recognize the truth of Swami will have to approach with tears of repentance and experience Me. Very soon, this will be worldwide.* **Swami is now restraining this development. When once it is allowed to manifest, the whole world will be transformed into Prasanthi Nilayam.**
>
> - Sathya Sai Speaks Volume 15 Chapter 55

May be the time is ripening now for such a world-scale development. So when Swami comes back He may not be bound by anything at all. There wouldn't be any need to. Swami has already lived a lifetime of 85 long years as a message and an example to all. Now it could be a second coming without any self-imposed inhibitions, invoking a full manifestation of omnipotence. Given all the clues that have come to light, whoever can count against such a possibility?

O Dear Lord Sathya Sai, Thy Kingdom come...

...Come may it soon!

Prayer

*Cherished Mother Sai,
We do Thee lovingly summon...*

*Thy will be done,
Thy Kingdom Come!*

*Do hear our plea, holding Thy
Lotus feet we pledge*

*And offer our all unto Thee,
We Thy children appeal to Thee...*

*Dark clouds cannot obliterate
the rays of the Sun for long*

*To shine upon Thy Kingdom,
the Sun too awaits its due...*

*To worship and adore Thee...
We seek moments anew!* [1]

---

[1] Prayer by Sri Jullie Chaudhuri

O Lord, take my love,
Let it flow in fullness of devotion to Thee;

O Lord, take my hands,
Let them work incessantly for Thee;

O Lord, take my soul,
Let it be merged in One with Thee;

O Lord, take my mind and thoughts,
Let them be in tune with Thee;

O Lord, take my everything,
Let me be an instrument to work for Thee.

Bibliography and References

- *An Eastern View of Jesus Christ*, Lee Hewlett and K. Nataraj, Sai Publications, 1982
- *Anyatha Saranam Nasthi (Other than You Refuge There is None)*, Smt. Vijayakumari, Sai Shriram Printers, 1999
- *Baba: Satya Sai*, Ra. Ganapati, Satya Jyoti, 12, Radhakrishnan Street, Madras, 600017, India, 1981
- *Bihar-ul-Anwar* Volume 13 Part 1 & 2, Allamah Muhammad Baqir al-Majlis, English Translation, Ja'fari Propagation Centre, Mumbai
- *Bhagavan Sri Sathya Sai Baba (An Interpretation)*, V.K.Gokak, New Delhi: Abhinav Publications, 1975
- *Conversations with Bhagavan Sri Sathya Sai Baba*, J.S.Hislop, Sri Sathya Sai Books & Publications Trust
- *Conversations with Sathya Sai Baba*, J.S.Hislop, Birth Day Publishing Co., San Diego, CA, 1978
- *God Descends on Earth*, Sanjay Kant, Sri Sathya Sai Towers Pvt. Ltd., 1998
- *In Search of Sai Divine*, Satya Pal Ruhela, M.D. Publications Pvt. Ltd., 1996
- KJV: *King James Version* of the Holy Bible
- *Living Divinity*, Shakuntala Balu, Sawbridge Enterprises, 1981
- *Modern Miracles: An Investigative Report on Psychic Phenomena Associated With Sathya Sai Baba*, Erlendur Haraldsson, Hastings House, 1997

- *My Baba and I*, Dr.John S. Hislop, Birth Day Publishing Co., 1985
- *My Beloved. The Love and Teaching of Bhagavan Sri Sathya Sai Baba*, Charles Penn, Sri Sathya Sai Baba Books and Publications Trust, Prasanthi Nilayam, 1981
- *Sacred Nadi Readings*, Compiled by Sri Vasantha Sai, Sri Vasantha Sai Books & Publications Trust, Mukthi Nilayam, 2011
- *Sai Baba and the Nara Narayan Gufa Ashram Part 1 & 2*, Swami Maheshwaranand, ed. B.P. Mishra. Bombay: Prasanthi Printers, 1990
- *Sai Baba Avatar: A New Journey into Power and Glory*, Howard Murphet, San Diego, Birth Day Publishing Co., 1977
- *Sai Baba, The Holy Man and the Psychiatrist*, Samuel H. Sandweiss, San Diego: Birth Day Publishing Co., 1975
- *Sai Messages for You and Me Vol. I.*, Lucas Ralli, London: Vridnavanum Books, 1985
- *Sai Messages for You and Me Vol. II.*, Lucas Ralli, London: Vridnavanum Books, 1988
- *Sai Vaani*: Messages collected from discourses of Sri Sathya Sai Baba
- *Sai Vandana*, ed. K.Hanumanthappa, Prasanthi Nilayam, Sri Sathya Sai Institute of Higher Learning, 1995
- *Sanathana Sarathi*: A monthly magazine published from Prasanthi Nilayam
- *Sathya Sai Baba, Embodiment of Love*, Peggy Mason and Ron Laing, London, Sawbridge, 1982

- *Sathya Sai Speaks*: Discourses by Bhagawan Sri Sathya Baba translated from Telugu (Sri Sathya Sai Books and Publication Trust)
- *Sathyam Sivam Sundaram* Volumes 1-4, Sri N.Kasturi, Sri Sathya Sai Books and Publications Trust, Prasanthi Nilayam, 1961-1980
- *Sri Sathya Sai Avathar*, V.Aravind Subramaniyam, Sura Books Pvt. Ltd., 2004
- *Sri Sathya Sai Baba and the Future of Mankind*, Sathya Pal Ruhela, New Delhi: Sai Kripa, 1991
- *Sri Sathya Sai Baba A Yugavatar*, Dr.K.Hanumanthappa, Sri Sathya Sai Books and Publications Trust, Prasanthi Nilayam, 2008
- *Thapovanam Sri Sathya Sai Sathcharithra*, Jandhyala Venkateswara Sastry, Sri Sathya Sai Books and Publications Trust, 2002
- *The Blitz Interview*: The extended interview given by Sri Sathya Sai Baba to the chief editor R.K.Karanjia of Blitz Magazine in September of 1976
- *The Heart of Sai*, R. Lowenberg, Sri Sathya Sai Towers Pvt. Ltd., 1981
- *The Life of Bhagavan Sri Sathya Sai Baba*, Kasturi.N, Sri Sathya Sai Baba Book Center of America, 1971

Humbly dedicated at His Divine Lotus Feet

*** JAI SAI RAM ***

Printed in Great Britain
by Amazon.co.uk, Ltd.,
Marston Gate.